Reading FORWARD

INTERMEDIATE 2

INTERMEDIATE 2

Series Editors Bin-na Yang, Dong-sook Kim

Project Editors Jung-ah Lee, Mina Song, Mi-youn Woo, Jee-young Song, Jin-young Song, Sung-ho Jun, Seol-mee Lee

Contributing Writers Patrick Ferraro, Henry John Amen IV, John Boswell, Robert Vernon, Alicja Serafin, Keeran Murphy, Peter Morton

Illustrators Seol-hee Kim, Hyun-jin Choi, Hyo-sil Lee, Da-som Kim

Design Ho-hyun Bang, Hyun-jung Jang, Yeon-joo Kim

Editorial Designer In-sun Lee

Sales Ki-young Han, Kyung-koo Lee, In-gyu Park, Cheol-gyo Jeong, Nam-jun Kim, Woo-hyun Lee

Marketers Hye-sun Park, Kyung-jin Nam, Ji-won Lee, Yeo-jin Kim

Copyright © 2015 by NE Neungyule, Inc.

First Printing 15 June 2015

12th Printing 15 July 2023

ISBN 979-11-253-0799-0 53740

INTRODUCTION

★
★
★ Reading Forward is a six-level series of three progressive steps: Basic, Intermediate, and Advanced. Based on the essential needs of young students, the series focuses on a specific goal: expanding vocabulary and knowledge. This goal guides all of the content and activities in the series. The first step of the series will enlarge vocabulary, and the later steps will increase knowledge. Thus, the series will eventually help students improve their reading comprehension.

Each book of Reading Forward is composed of 20 units. The number of words used in each reading passage is as follows.

Step 3
Reading Forward
Advanced
for Knowledge
1 : 240 – 260 words
2 : 260 – 280 words

Step 2
Reading Forward
Intermediate
for Vocabulary & Knowledge
1 : 200 – 220 words
2 : 220 – 240 words

Step 1
Reading Forward
Basic
for Vocabulary
1 : 150 – 170 words
2 : 170 – 190 words

Key Features of Reading Forward Series

– Current, high-interest topics are developed in an easy way so that students can understand them. These subjects can hold their attention and keep them motivated to read forward.

– Comprehension checkup questions presented in the series are based on standardized test questions. These can help students prepare for English tests at school, as well as official English language tests.

– Each unit is designed to expand vocabulary and knowledge by presenting newly created sections: English Dictionary, Encyclopedia Contents related to the main topic. Students will be intrigued by this intellectual content and eventually build the basics of improved reading comprehension.

FORMAT

Before Reading

The question before each passage allows students to think about the topic by relating it to their lives. It also helps students become interested in the passage before reading it.

Reading

This part serves as the main passage of the unit, and it explains an intriguing and instructive topic in great depth. As students progress through the book, the content of these passages becomes more and more substantial.

Reading Comprehension

The reading is followed by different types of questions, which test understanding of the passage. The various types of questions focus on important reading skills, such as understanding the main idea and organization of the passage, identifying details, and drawing inferences.

Strategic Summary / Organizer

Each unit includes a strategic summary or organizer of the main reading passage. It gives students a better understanding of the important points and organization of the passage. These exercises focus on further development of effective reading comprehension skills.

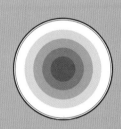

Knowledge Expanding

Each unit provides one of three different forms in Knowledge Expanding: Encyclopedia Contents, English Dictionary, and a further reading passage. These are related to the topic of the main passage, and thus it allows students to explore the topic in depth and expand their vocabulary.

Vocabulary Review

A review of the key vocabulary concludes each unit. Three types of exercises test understanding of new words: matching definitions, identifying synonyms and antonyms, and completing sentences with the correct words in context.

TABLE OF CONTENTS

★ ★ ★ ★ ★

Reading Forward

Before Reading
If you lost everything in a big fire, how would you feel?

Chicago City Planning

A fire burns things to ashes. This means everything can be lost in a fire. However, a fire can also create an opportunity
5 to start something new. This is what happened a long time ago in Chicago.

One October night in 1871, the Great Fire of Chicago
10 started. It happened suddenly, but it could have been predicted. For 40 years before the fire, Chicago had grown quickly with very little planning.
15 (①) Many of the buildings and streets were made of wood. (②) Furthermore, the summer of 1871 had been very dry. (③) Blown by a strong wind, it moved through the center of the city. (④) Two days after the fire began, about 18,000 buildings had been destroyed, and 300 people had died.

20 The fire destroyed a third of Chicago, but this was not the end of the city. Right after the fire, 50 million dollars was raised to rebuild the city. This time, the buildings were constructed with plenty of planning. The best architects and engineers were hired to build a new, modern city. _____(A)_____, the latest steel frame techniques and innovative
25 construction methods were used. Thanks to this modern technology, some of the world's first skyscrapers were built in Chicago. They give Chicago its unique skyline and beauty.

Today, a lot of tourists go to visit Chicago. But, very few of them know that this beautiful city has truly risen from the ashes.

1 What is the best title for the passage?

  a. How to Prevent a Fire
  b. A City Built from Its Ashes
  c. The Beauty of Modern Chicago
  d. How Architecture Has Developed

2 Where would the following sentence best fit?

> So, when a fire began in a barn, it quickly spread out of control.

  a. ①   b. ②   c. ③   d. ④

3 What is NOT mentioned about the Great Fire of Chicago?

  a. When it broke out
  b. What caused it to spread so fast
  c. How much it damaged the city
  d. How people could have stopped it sooner

4 What is the best choice for blank (A)?

  a. However   b. Instead
  c. For example   d. In addition

5 By using the latest steel frame techniques and innovative construction methods, _____.

6 What is the best pair for blanks (A) and (B)?

> The Great Fire changed Chicago from a(n) __(A)__ city to a(n) __(B)__ city.

	(A)		(B)
a.	rich	—	poor
b.	fast-growing	—	ordinary
c.	industrial	—	sightseeing
d.	unplanned	—	well-planned

STRATEGIC SUMMARY

Fill in the blanks with the correct words.

Before the Great Fire of Chicago _____ in 1871, the city had grown very quickly with little planning. Many of its buildings were made of wood. This, along with strong winds, helped the fire _____ throughout the city. A third of Chicago was destroyed, but people used this as a chance to _____ the city for the better. There was much planning, and modern _____ techniques were used. The result was a beautiful, modern city with some of the world's first skyscrapers. This beauty can still be seen in Chicago today.

| construction | broke out | rebuild | ashes | spread |

★ EXPANDING KNOWLEDGE ★

Encyclopedia Contents: City Planning

1. Main concerns
   1.1 The use of land
   1.2 Design of the urban environment
2. Aspects
   2.1 Aesthetics
   2.2 Safety and security
   2.3 Transportation
   2.4 Environmental protection
   2.5 Water and sanitation

3. Structures
   3.1 Buildings
      3.1.1 Residential buildings
      3.1.2 Non-residential buildings
   3.2 Transportation
      3.2.1 Road and highway
      3.2.2 Public transportation
   3.3 Utilities
      3.3.1 Water, gas, electricity, etc.
      3.3.2 Waste and sewage
          treatment

1 Write the correct highlighted word next to its definition.

1) used as a place to live: _____

2) relating to cities and towns: _____

3) a system for carrying passengers from one place to another: _____

2 Write T if the statement is true or F if it's false.

1) The beauty of the city isn't a matter of concern in city planning.

2) City planning includes designing sewage disposal facilities.

—— *Unit ⋆ 01* ——
VOCABULARY REVIEW

A Write the correct word next to its definition.

ash	barn	skyline	skyscraper	construct

1 the shape made by buildings against the sky: _____

2 the gray powder that is left when something is burned: _____

3 to build or make something such as a building, bridge, or road: _____

4 a large building on a farm for storing crops or keeping animals: _____

B Find the word that has a similar meaning to the underlined word.

1 The company <u>hired</u> 500 new workers this year.

   a. invited   *b.* fired   *c.* employed   *d.* praised

2 They will hold a concert to <u>raise</u> money for charity.

   a. draw   *b.* collect   *c.* destroy   *d.* increase

C Choose the best word to complete each sentence.

1 It's hard to _____ what will happen in the future.

   a. reserve   *b.* forget   *c.* predict   *d.* contract

2 Don't rub the stain on your carpet, or it will _____.

   a. burn   *b.* appear   *c.* spread   *d.* move

3 To succeed in the field of technology, you need _____ ideas.

   a. electric   *b.* innovative   *c.* disposable   *d.* depressing

4 A(n) _____ is a person whose job is to design buildings.

   a. translator   *b.* agent   *c.* publisher   *d.* architect

Before Reading

Have you ever seen the movie *The Pirates of the Caribbean*?

The Caribbean Pirates

Have you ever seen a picture of a human skull and crossbones? Today, it suggests that something is poisonous. But for Caribbean sailors in the 18th century, it was the symbol for pirates! So where did these pirates come from?

After Columbus discovered the Caribbean islands in 1492, many Europeans went there in search of wealth and to establish colonies. The strongest power was Spain, but people from other countries settled down there, too. Among them were some French

10 people who lived on Hispaniola Island, one of the Caribbean islands. (①) They hunted pigs and cattle on the island and sold the dried meat to passing ships. (②) So, the Spanish chased them from Hispaniola, which made them hate the Spanish. (③) They went to another island and joined British and Dutch sailors. (④) Soon, they became pirates who attacked the Spanish!

15 Meanwhile, countries like England found that using pirates was a cheap and effective way to attack their rival, Spain. So they hired pirates to attack the Spanish ships and colonies. However, as the pirates got stronger, they became hard to control, and they even caused

20 unwanted wars. Eventually, European countries
_____(A)_____ and built their navies to protect their colonies.

There aren't any pirates in the Caribbean today. But <u>you can see them in books,</u>

25 <u>movies, and cartoons</u>. You can also see them in the logo of a baseball team, the Pittsburgh Pirates!

1 What is the best title for the passage?

a. The History of Piracy in the Caribbean

b. Columbus' Discovery of the New World

c. The Hard Lives of Sailors in the Caribbean

d. The Caribbean Islands: A Place You Must Visit

2 What did the picture of a skull and crossbones mean for Caribbean sailors in the 18th century?

_____

3 Where would the following sentence best fit?

But they also attacked and stole the ships!

a. ①   b. ②   c. ③   d. ④

4 What is the best choice for blank (A)?

a. made piracy illegal

b. fought for freedom

c. left the New World

d. joined the Spanish navy

5 What can be inferred from the underlined part?

a. Pirates existed only in our imaginations.

b. Pirates are used in many works of fiction.

c. Pirates have become famous entertainers.

d. Pirates are popular because of their friendly image.

6 What is NOT true about the Caribbean pirates?

a. They were originally French people who lived on Hispaniola Island.

b. They once hunted pigs and cattle on Hispaniola Island.

c. They consisted of only French settlers.

d. England used them to attack Spanish ships.

Fill in the blanks with the correct words.

The Caribbean Pirates

- Were originally French people who lived on Hispaniola Island _____ and selling pigs and cattle
- Were _____ off the island by the Spanish
- Became pirates and began attacking the Spanish
- Were used by England to attack England's _____, Spain
- Became _____ because European countries couldn't control them

| rival | illegal | sailors | chased | hunting |

★ EXPANDING KNOWLEDGE ★

Encyclopedia Contents: Caribbean

1. Composition
   1.1 The Caribbean Sea
   1.2 The Caribbean islands: about 700 islands
2. Origin: "Caribs," native American groups
3. Location
   3.1 East of Central America
   3.2 North of South America

4. Official languages
   4.1 Spanish, French, English, Dutch, etc.
   4.2 Background: colonization by European countries
5. Climate: tropical weather
   5.1 Average temperature: 27°C
   5.2 Dry and wet seasons

1 Write the correct highlighted word next to its definition.

1) approved of by proper authority: _____

2) the typical weather conditions of a particular area: _____

3) relating to the people who originally lived in an area: _____

2 Write T if the statement is true or F if it's false.

1) The word "Caribbean" comes from people who moved from Europe.

2) Various languages in the Caribbean are related to the history of colonization.

VOCABULARY REVIEW

A Write the correct word next to its definition.

logo	hunt	skull	pirate	colony

1 to run after animals to kill or catch them: _____

2 a small design that is the official symbol of an organization: _____

3 a country or area that is controlled politically by another country: _____

4 the bone that forms a person or animal's head and surrounds the brain: _____

B Find the word that has the opposite meaning of the underlined word.

1 Melanie is the type of person who <u>hates</u> losing.

    a. dislikes   *b.* knows   *c.* hopes   *d.* loves

2 I'd like to <u>settle down</u> in the countryside after I retire.

    a. arrive   *b.* come   *c.* leave   *d.* root

C Choose the best word to complete each sentence.

1 Mickey Mouse is a famous _____ character.

    a. folktale   *b.* poem   *c.* cartoon   *d.* horror

2 Barking loudly, the dog _____ off the thief.

    a. showed   *b.* chased   *c.* turned   *d.* put

3 Putting on your seat belt will _____ you against injury.

    a. damage   *b.* protect   *c.* harm   *d.* treat

4 The new cold medicine is more _____ than the old one.

    a. boring   *b.* complicated   *c.* creative   *d.* effective

Pop Art

If you visit the Museum of Modern Art in New York, you will find a painting of 32 ordinary soup cans. ① It is very simple, so you probably wouldn't consider it anything special. ② However, you may be surprised to learn that it is worth more than 11 million dollars! ③ The true value of artwork isn't related to money at all. ④ Actually, it is one of the most famous pieces of pop art ever created.

Pop art is short for popular art. It refers to art that focuses on popular culture. It began in the 1950s in Britain and the U.S., and then spread around the world. Pop art focuses on _____(A)_____, such as celebrities, advertisements, comic

15 books, movies, and television shows. There are a number of famous pop artists, including Andy Warhol and Roy Lichtenstein. Warhol is known for using images of famous people and things, often copying them and changing their colors. Meanwhile, Lichtenstein is known for his paintings that were inspired by cartoons.

20 Pop art is exciting and popular because it offers a totally new, fresh look at daily life. Traditionally, art was considered something that was elite and had nothing to do with ordinary things. However, pop art challenges this idea. It turns the images people see in daily life into something artistic and interesting.

25 That's why the work of pop artists appeals to everyone. Clearly, thanks to pop art, art has become more familiar to the public!

1 What is the best title for the passage?

    a. How to Enjoy Pop Art

    b. Pop Art: Art for the Elite

    c. Pop Art: Art from Daily Life

    d. The Famous Works of Pop Art

2 Which sentence is NOT needed in the passage?

    a. ①   *b.* ②   *c.* ③   *d.* ④

3 What is the best choice for blank (A)?

    a. strange topics

    b. classical objects

    c. boring materials

    d. everyday subjects

4 Before pop art became popular, art had been thought of as

_____.

5 What is NOT mentioned about pop art?

    a. Where it began

    b. What artists were involved

    c. Why it has been popular

    d. When it ended

6 Write T if the statement is true or F if it's false.

    1) Lichtenstein is famous for his works that use images of celebrities.

    2) Pop art is different from traditional art because of its fresh view on daily life.

Fill in the blanks with the correct words.

In the 1950s, pop art started in Britain and the U.S. and changed the way we look at everyday objects. Artists such as Andy Warhol and Roy Lichtenstein created art inspired by people or things taken from popular culture, including _____, comics, and movies. Pop art has _____ the elite ideas of traditional art and has provided a fresh and exciting look at the _____ things we see in our daily lives. The fact that everyone can relate to pop art is the key to its _____.

popularity   adopted   celebrities   common   challenged

★ EXPANDING KNOWLEDGE ★

The artist Andy Warhol was born in 1928 and had his first one-man show at the age of 27. In 1956, he was part of a major exhibition at New York's Museum of Modern Art. But his real success came in the 1960s. He became famous for creating images of people and things from popular culture, like Marilyn Monroe and cans of Campbell's soup. His fame was also strengthened by his strange personal life. He spent money freely, liked to hang out with rich people, and wore unusual clothes. Warhol died in 1987, but he is still remembered as the "Prince of Pop Art."

1 What is the best title for the passage?

   a. The Origin of Pop Art

   b. The Popularity of Pop Art

   c. The Life Story of Andy Warhol

   d. Andy Warhol and His Rich Friends

2 Write T if the statement is true or F if it's false.

   1) Warhol became famous for his relationship with Marilyn Monroe.

   2) Though Warhol is dead, he is still remembered as a great pop artist.

VOCABULARY REVIEW

A Write the correct word next to its definition.

challenge	focus	appeal	inspire	elite

1 being the best of its kind: _____

2 to attract or interest someone: _____

3 to give somebody the idea for something: _____

4 to give special attention to a certain person or thing: _____

B Find the word that has the opposite meaning of the underlined word.

1 His ideas on music education are pretty <u>fresh</u>.

    a. creative   *b.* weird   *c.* unique   *d.* old-fashioned

2 I was glad to see many <u>familiar</u> faces at the party last night.

    a. simple   *b.* friendly   *c.* artistic   *d.* strange

C Choose the best word to complete each sentence.

1 He is a(n) _____ student who doesn't stand out from others.

    a. unusual   *b.* ordinary   *c.* distinct   *d.* noticeable

2 The picture drawn by Van Gogh is _____ millions of dollars.

    a. useful   *b.* valueless   *c.* important   *d.* worth

3 We call a famous person, especially in the entertainment business, a _____.

    a. celebrity   *b.* politician   *c.* career   *d.* professional

4 The _____ displayed in this museum was made in 19th-century Europe.

    a. value   *b.* success   *c.* artwork   *d.* popularity

04 LITERATURE

Before Reading

Have you read the story of a man named Jean Valjean?

Jean Valjean

One day, a bishop received a visit from a poor stranger named Jean Valjean. The next morning, he was in his study when he heard
5 *his servant calling him.*

"Bishop! The stranger is gone and so is our silverware! He must have stolen it!" cried the servant. The bishop thought for a moment and
10 sighed. "Did the silverware really belong to us?" he asked. "I think it belongs to whoever needs it most. And obviously a poor person would need it more than I
15 do. Is it really wrong that he took it?"

Just then there was a knock on the door. When the bishop opened it, he saw three police officers holding Jean Valjean. The bishop smiled and greeted Jean. "There you are! You left in such a hurry. You forgot the silver candlesticks I gave you!" Jean stared at the bishop in shock. The
20 police officers also looked surprised. "So, he was telling the truth?" asked one. "When we saw him running down the street with a bag of silverware, we assumed he was a thief." "I'm afraid there has been a mistake," said the bishop. "Please let him go."

After the police officers left, Jean approached the bishop. His whole
25 body was trembling. "Is it true? Am I free to go?" he asked. "Yes," said the bishop. "But, don't forget to use the money from this silverware to become an honest man." Jean was so grateful that he was unable to think of anything to say.

1 What is the best title for the passage?

    a. The Arrest of Jean Valjean

    b. The Bishop's Special Candlesticks

    c. Why Jean Valjean Became a Thief

    d. The Bishop's Kindness to Jean Valjean

2 Why did the bishop mention the underlined sentence in the 1st paragraph?

    a. To order his servant to find Jean Valjean

    b. To ask if Jean Valjean took the silverware

    c. To emphasize what Jean Valjean did was wrong

    d. To say it is okay for Jean Valjean to have the silverware

3 The underlined sentence in the 2nd paragraph suggests that Jean Valjean

_____.

    a. didn't want to take the candlesticks

    b. knew that the bishop would treat him kindly

    c. said that he was going to the bishop's house

    d. said the bishop had given the silverware to him

4 What can be inferred from the 2nd paragraph?

    a. The bishop couldn't remember Jean Valjean.

    b. The bishop tried to hide Jean Valjean's theft.

    c. Jean Valjean wanted to return the silverware to the bishop.

    d. The police officers didn't know that Jean Valjean was a thief.

5 What did the bishop want Jean Valjean to do with the silverware?

_____

6 What is NOT true about the passage?

    a. The servant thought that Jean Valjean stole the silverware.

    b. Jean Valjean returned the silver candlesticks to the bishop.

    c. Jean Valjean didn't expect the bishop to greet him the way he did.

    d. Jean Valjean was thankful for what the bishop did for him.

Fill in the blanks with the correct words.

A poor stranger named Jean Valjean spent a night in a bishop's house. During the night, he _____ some silverware. Instead of getting angry, the bishop said the silverware _____ whoever needed it most. Later, three police officers brought Jean Valjean to the bishop because they _____ he was a thief. But the bishop said he gave the silverware to Jean Valjean and made them let him go. He then told Jean Valjean to use the money from the silverware to become a(n) _____ man.

stole	visited	honest	assumed	belonged to

★ EXPANDING KNOWLEDGE ★

Les Miserables, which means "the miserable ones" in English, is a famous 19th-century novel written by the great French novelist and poet Victor Hugo. It tells the story of a thief named Jean Valjean. He goes to prison for 19 years for stealing bread. After his release, he is full of anger toward the world. _____(A)_____, after being saved from police by a bishop, he decides to be an honest man. Finally, he becomes wealthy and successful. He also saves an innocent man and raises a poor young girl as his daughter. The novel reminds us to think again about goodness and social injustice.

1 What is the best choice for blank (A)?

    a. However   *b.* In addition

    c. Likewise   *d.* For example

2 Write T if the statement is true or F if it's false.

    1) Jean Valjean was in prison because he stole bread.

    2) Jean Valjean did many good deeds, though he was poor his whole life.

VOCABULARY REVIEW

A Write the correct word next to its definition.

greet	thief	honest	grateful	approach

1 feeling or expressing thanks: _____

2 someone who steals something: _____

3 to move near or nearer to somebody or something: _____

4 always telling the truth, and not cheating or stealing: _____

B Find the word that has a similar meaning to the underlined word.

1 He always does his best. He is <u>obviously</u> an excellent student.

    a. generally   *b.* certainly   *c.* surprisingly   *d.* accidentally

2 I <u>assume</u> that he is a Southerner, based on his accent.

    a. think   *b.* tell   *c.* advise   *d.* persuade

C Choose the best word to complete each sentence.

1 She ordered her _____ to clean up the entire house.

    a. services   *b.* materials   *c.* servants   *d.* mistakes

2 Looking at his poor grade on the exam, he _____.

    a. cured   *b.* sighed   *c.* behaved   *d.* relaxed

3 Everyone _____ at the waitress when she dropped the plates.

    a. stared   *b.* suffered   *c.* wondered   *d.* whispered

4 His hands were _____ while he stood on the stage.

    a. afraid   *b.* exciting   *c.* trembling   *d.* threatening

FESTIVALS

Las Fallas

Gray smoke filled the air! I smelled burnt gunpowder everywhere I went. I was in Valencia, Spain, enjoying Las Fallas! Las Fallas,

5 which means "the fires" in Valencian, is one of the biggest festivals in Spain. It was started to celebrate St. Joseph, the saint of carpenters.

10   During the five days before St. Joseph's Day, which is on March 19th, there were many parades, musical performances, and street parties. Also, at 2 p.m. every afternoon, a fireworks display was held. People

15 were throwing firecrackers in the street. I could feel my body shake from the powerful sounds!

    The highlight of the festival was the burning of the ninots. Ninots are large dolls made of paper and wood. They resemble many different things, such as dragons, mermaids, and angels. They were so huge that I felt like I

20 was in the book *Gulliver's Travels*! To my surprise, some were even 20 meters tall! The tradition of burning ninots comes from the Middle Ages. In those days, carpenters used to burn their wooden candle holders to welcome the spring. Later, this practice was done on St. Joseph's Day. Today, people burn ninots instead of the candle holders.

    As the ninots were set on fire, the biggest flame I'd ever seen rose up into the sky! It was a little sad to see such beautiful artwork turn to ashes, but it left me with my most impressive memory of Spain.

1 What is the best title for the passage?

   a. Big Fires in Valencia, Spain

   b. Las Fallas: The Festival of Fires

   c. Las Fallas for Modern Carpenters

   d. Ninots: Beautiful Artwork in Spain

2 What were people doing at 2 p.m. every afternoon during Las Fallas?

_____

3 Why does the writer mention the book *Gulliver's Travels*?

   a. To emphasize how big the ninots were

   b. To show how interesting the ninots were

   c. To explain that Valencia is the setting of *Gulliver's Travels*

   d. To say many ninots resemble characters from *Gulliver's Travels*

4 Today, people burn ninots to _____.

   a. honor the best fireworks display of the year

   b. follow a tradition performed to greet the spring

   c. remember how St. Joseph burned candle holders

   d. show that carpenters hope to make greater works

5 What is NOT mentioned about Las Fallas?

   a. Who started it

   b. When it is held

   c. What events take place

   d. What its highlight is

6 Write T if the statement is true or F if it's false.

   1) Ninots are large wooden candle holders.

   2) The writer felt sad when he saw the ninots burning.

Fill in the blanks with the correct words.

Las Fallas is a major festival held each March in Valencia, Spain. It was originally begun to _____ St. Joseph's Day. For five days during Las Fallas, there are parades, musical _____, parties, and fireworks displays. But the main event is the _____ of the ninots. These are huge dolls that are burnt to welcome spring. It is a really impressive sight to watch such beautiful _____ set on fire!

> performances   burning   tradition   artwork   celebrate

★ EXPANDING KNOWLEDGE ★

English Dictionary	fire			▼	Search

Related Search	spark explosion	flash crime	torch victim	glow fuel	burn

Synonyms
1. (a burning)   • blaze   • flame   • flare
2. (a strong feeling)   • enthusiasm   • passion

Collocations from the first sense
• a fire alarm
• a disastrous fire
• a fire extinguisher
• put out a fire
• a forest fire

Write the correct highlighted word next to its definition.

1 an illegal activity: _____

2 a device used to put out fires: _____

3 intense excitement about something: _____

4 substance like oil or coal that is burned to produce power: _____

VOCABULARY REVIEW

A Write the correct word next to its definition.

| flame | ash | celebrate | highlight | carpenter |

1 someone whose job is to build objects from wood: _____

2 the most important or enjoyable part of something: _____

3 to do something special to recognize an important event: _____

4 the bright burning gas that is produced when something is on fire: _____

B Find the word that has a similar meaning to the underlined word.

1 It was amazing to see such <u>huge</u> planes take off so easily.

    a. tiny   *b.* fat   *c.* large   *d.* fast

2 It is common <u>practice</u> in Korea to take off your shoes when you enter a house.

    a. action   *b.* custom   *c.* belief   *d.* information

C Choose the best word to complete each sentence.

1 Steve and James _____ each other. I can't tell who's who.

    a. resemble   *b.* respect   *c.* create   *d.* shake

2 His success story is _____. I want to be a writer like him.

    a. narrow   *b.* scary   *c.* impressive   *d.* generous

3 The child was the _____ of the hit-and-run accident last night.

    a. director   *b.* participant   *c.* referee   *d.* victim

4 This backpack trip will leave them with unforgettable _____.

    a. contests   *b.* memories   *c.* talents   *d.* tricks

Maple Syrup

Have you ever seen the Canadian flag? In the middle of it, there's a big red maple leaf. It was chosen to be the symbol of Canada because there are lots of maple trees all across the country. Canadians use them for
5 many things, like making delicious maple syrup!

Maple syrup has been a part of Canadian culture for hundreds of years. It was first made by native people living in the Northeast. Nowadays, about 85 percent of the world's maple syrup comes
10 from Canada. Canadians love maple syrup so much that they eat it with waffles, pancakes, oatmeal, and baked goods, and they even add it to beer.

This popular syrup is made by boiling *sap, which is collected from maple trees. The sap contains about 3 percent
15 sugar and a lot of water. It gets thicker and sweeter as the water boils away. When it contains about 66 percent sugar, it becomes syrup! Syrup that's not produced this way or includes artificial maple flavoring can't be called maple syrup.

In Canada, freshly made syrup is classified according to
20 _____(A)_____, from grade 1 to grade 3. The higher the number, the darker the syrup! Light-colored syrup is usually used for making candy, and dark-colored syrup is recommended for baking or cooking. If you haven't eaten maple syrup yet, be sure to try it on pancakes. Then you'll understand why Canadians love it so much!

*sap: a watery substance in trees and plants

1 What is the best title for the passage?

  a. The Symbol of the Canadian Flag
  b. The Long History of Canadian Culture
  c. Maple Syrup: A Sweet Canadian Treat
  d. The Excellence of Artificial Maple Flavoring

2 Why did the maple leaf become the symbol of Canada?

_____

3 What can be inferred from the underlined part?

  a. The process of making syrup is very complicated.
  b. Maple syrup is so sweet that water should be added to it.
  c. High-quality maple syrup is made by adding a lot of sugar.
  d. Maple syrup is made by increasing the percentage of sugar in the sap.

4 What is the best choice for blank (A)?

  a. its price
  b. its color
  c. its quality
  d. its purpose

5 What is NOT mentioned about Canadian maple syrup?

  a. Who made it first
  b. How it is used
  c. How it is made
  d. How to choose the best syrup

6 Write T if the statement is true or F if it's false.

  1) Canada produces the greatest amount of maple syrup in the world.
  2) All syrup that has maple flavoring in it can be called maple syrup.

Fill in the blanks with the correct words.

Maple Syrup

- First made by _____ Canadians hundreds of years ago
- Eaten with various foods
- Produced from maple sap, which is _____ from maple trees
- Made to contain at least 66 percent sugar by _____ the sap
- _____ into 3 grades according to its color

> classified   boiling   native   collected   thick

★ EXPANDING KNOWLEDGE ★

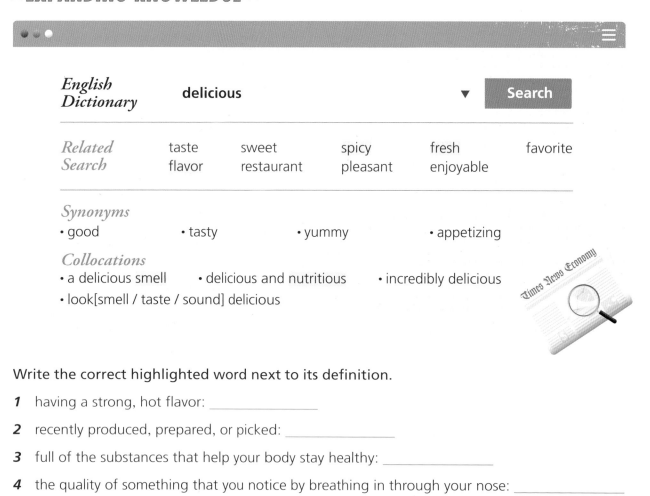

| *English Dictionary* | **delicious** | | | ▼ | **Search** |

| *Related Search* | taste | sweet | spicy | fresh | favorite |
| | flavor | restaurant | pleasant | enjoyable | |

Synonyms
- good   • tasty   • yummy   • appetizing

Collocations
- a delicious smell   • delicious and nutritious   • incredibly delicious
- look[smell / taste / sound] delicious

Write the correct highlighted word next to its definition.

1 having a strong, hot flavor: _____

2 recently produced, prepared, or picked: _____

3 full of the substances that help your body stay healthy: _____

4 the quality of something that you notice by breathing in through your nose: _____

VOCABULARY REVIEW

A Write the correct word next to its definition.

grade	maple	symbol	artificial	flavoring

1 not natural; made or done by people: _____

2 a shape that represents an organization, country, or idea: _____

3 a tree with star-like leaves that turn red or yellow in the fall: _____

4 something added to a drink or food to give it a particular taste: _____

B Find the word that has a similar meaning to the underlined word.

1 With this machine, it became possible to <u>produce</u> a car in minutes.

   a. make   *b.* expect   *c.* provide   *d.* demand

2 Soft drinks can be unhealthy because most of them <u>contain</u> caffeine.

   a. allow   *b.* include   *c.* describe   *d.* consume

C Choose the best word to complete each sentence.

1 Water _____ at 100 degrees Celsius.

   a. boils   *b.* freezes   *c.* increases   *d.* disappears

2 Taking sleeping pills often is not _____ by doctors.

   a. used   *b.* prepared   *c.* punished   *d.* recommended

3 Add more water if the soup is too _____.

   a. light   *b.* clear   *c.* thick   *d.* delicious

4 The zoologist _____ the animals according to their species.

   a. promised   *b.* respected   *c.* delivered   *d.* classified

Before Reading
Have you ever thought about what happens to old planes?

The Airplane Graveyard

When people die, they're buried in a graveyard. But where do airplanes go when they are no longer used? One place is the

5 Mojave Desert's airplane graveyard in California. It's a resting place for hundreds of planes that have been retired from service.

So where do these planes

10 come from? Mostly from major airlines. They are sent to the Mojave because airlines won't need them for some time or maybe ever again. Some planes only stay

15 a few months, while others stay there for years. But not all of them are truly "dead." Some planes get a chance to start a second life as cargo aircraft. And a few of them go back to passenger service. Of course, they have to be carefully tested to make sure they are safe. Others may sometimes be used to replace parts for planes that are still flying.

20 Although it's strange to see so many giant airplanes sitting in the middle of the desert, the Mojave is the perfect place for them. This is because it's very dry and clear, so the planes aren't damaged by the weather. Also, the ground in the Mojave is naturally very hard. So it can easily support the weight of the huge

25 planes.

The wide desert and the old planes give this place an exotic look. Thanks to this scenery, the Mojave's airplane graveyard has appeared in many movies, and tourists travel there to see the planes.

1 What is the best title for the passage?

    a. Different Types of Airplanes

    b. A Special Place for Retired Planes

    c. How to Travel Safely in the Desert

    d. The Mojave Desert: A Popular Tourist Spot

2 Why do many airlines send planes to the Mojave Desert?

_____

3 Why does the writer mention cargo aircraft?

    a. To name one of the major airlines

    b. To explain the features of modern planes

    c. To give an example of how planes are reused

    d. To list the types of planes buried in the desert

4 What makes the Mojave Desert the perfect storage area for the planes? (Choose two.)

    a. Its dry, clear weather

    b. Its wide, cheap land

    c. Its small population

    d. Its hard ground

5 What is NOT mentioned about the airplane graveyard?

    a. Where it is located

    b. How long the planes stay there

    c. What its planes are used for

    d. How many tourists visit there each year

6 Write T if the statement is true or F if it's false.

    1) Many of the planes in the graveyard belonged to major airlines.

    2) None of the planes in the graveyard will ever fly again.

STRATEGIC SUMMARY

Fill in the blanks with the correct words.

Many _____ planes are taken to an airplane graveyard in the Mojave Desert. Most of them are sent to this area by major airlines. While some stay there forever, others will be used again as cargo aircraft. A few even go back into service to _____ passengers after careful safety testing. The rest are sometimes used for _____ parts. The Mojave Desert is perfect for keeping aircraft because of its dry, clear _____ and hard ground. It's amazing to see so many old planes in one place.

> carry   retired   climate   replacement   strange

★ EXPANDING KNOWLEDGE ★

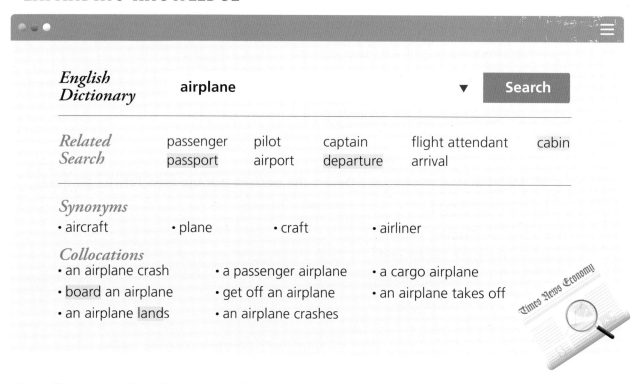

English Dictionary

airplane   ▼   **Search**

Related Search

| passenger | pilot | captain | flight attendant | cabin |
| passport | airport | departure | arrival | |

Synonyms
- aircraft
- plane
- craft
- airliner

Collocations
- an airplane crash
- a passenger airplane
- a cargo airplane
- board an airplane
- get off an airplane
- an airplane takes off
- an airplane lands
- an airplane crashes

Write the correct highlighted word next to its definition.

1 to get on or into a vehicle: _____

2 the act of leaving to travel somewhere: _____

3 to come down to the ground through the air: _____

4 an area inside a plane where the passengers sit: _____

Unit 07
VOCABULARY REVIEW

A Write the correct word next to its definition.

appear	cargo	major	retire	aircraft

1 a plane or any vehicle that can fly: _____

2 to be on television or in a film, play, concert, etc.: _____

3 to remove someone or something from a job or service: _____

4 the goods that are carried on a large vehicle, such as a ship or plane: _____

B Find the word that has a similar meaning to the underlined word.

1 My computer is too slow, so I think I have to replace it.

    a. repay   *b.* change   *c.* appoint   *d.* identify

2 It's surprising that she lives in that giant house alone.

    a. old   *b.* tiny   *c.* haunted   *d.* enormous

C Choose the best word to complete each sentence.

1 She doesn't eat anything at night in order to lose _____.

    a. height   *b.* weight   *c.* time   *d.* wrinkles

2 The soldier was killed in the war and _____ in the National Cemetery.

    a. biased   *b.* bowed   *c.* buried   *d.* burst

3 All of the _____ should be on the airplane in 10 minutes.

    a. percentages   *b.* passports   *c.* passwords   *d.* passengers

4 The house was greatly _____ by the typhoon that hit the region last night.

    a. grown   *b.* damaged   *c.* developed   *d.* renovated

Before Reading
Have you ever gone bowling? If you have, did you like it?

Bowling

Strike! It's exciting when your ball knocks down all the pins. Bowling looks like a modern sport, but you may be surprised to learn that it has thousands of years of history. It is believed that the first form of bowling was started in ancient Egypt.

5 Around 300 A.D., bowling reappeared in Germany. At that time, it was a religious ceremony held by priests. They bowled using a round rock and several wooden pins on a long lane. The priests thought of the pins as devils and the rock as a weapon to keep them away. They believed that if they knocked down all the pins, all their sins would be forgiven.

10 As time passed, bowling was introduced to people outside the church. But this time it was considered _____(A)_____! Everyone liked to bowl. It was so popular that it spread across Europe and then to other countries as well. Even Martin Luther, a famous reformer, was a big fan of it, and he set the number of pins at nine.

15 As bowling gained popularity, however, it started to cause problems. In England, for example, soldiers often neglected their duties because of bowling, so King Edward III banned it. (①) Later, in America, people started bowling not only for fun, but also to gamble on the games. (②) As a result, bowling became illegal. (③) That's how modern ten-pin bowling began!
20 (④) Today, it is one of the most popular sports in the world.

Edward III

36

1 What is the best title for the passage?

    a. How to Bowl

    b. The Popularity of Bowling

    c. The Origin of Modern Bowling

    d. The Most Popular Sport in Germany

2 What did German priests believe happened when they knocked down all the pins?

    _____

3 What is the best choice for blank (A)?

    a. education

    b. self-control

    c. entertainment

    d. military training

4 Where would the following sentence best fit?

> But as the law prohibited only nine-pin bowling, people added a tenth pin to get around this law.

    a. ①   *b.* ②   *c.* ③   *d.* ④

5 What is NOT mentioned about bowling?

    a. Where it first started

    b. Who used to play it

    c. What problems it caused

    d. Who established its modern rules

6 Write T if the statement is true or F if it's false.

    1) The pins German priests used at religious ceremonies represented devils.

    2) King Edward III allowed soldiers to bowl whenever they wanted.

Fill in the blanks with the correct words.

The modern sport of bowling is believed to have begun in ancient Egypt. Around 300 A.D., German priests believed that if they knocked down all the pins, their sins would be _____. Later, it was introduced to common people, and they did it for fun. Even Martin Luther enjoyed it, and he set the number of pins at nine. However, bowling was later _____ in both England and America because of the problems caused by its _____. This led to the development of modern ten-pin bowling. People in America _____ an extra pin to get around the law that made bowling illegal.

added	banned	forgiven	difference	popularity

★ EXPANDING KNOWLEDGE ★

English Dictionary	popularity			▼	Search

Related Search	famous	well-known	attention	fashionable
	attraction	trendy	celebrity	public

Synonyms
• fame   • reputation   • renown

Collocations
• enormous[huge] popularity   • maintain popularity   • lose popularity
• a decline in popularity   • a rise in popularity

Write the correct highlighted word next to its definition.

1 a famous person, usually an entertainer: _____

2 following the popular fashion or ideas of the day: _____

3 a feature that makes something interesting or desirable: _____

4 a decrease in the quality, quantity, value, etc. of something: _____

VOCABULARY REVIEW

A Write the correct word next to its definition.

sin	ban	priest	weapon	neglect

1 to refuse to allow by law: _____

2 an object used to fight, such as a sword or gun: _____

3 not to give someone or something enough care or attention: _____

4 a person who performs religious duties and ceremonies in a church: _____

B Find the word that has a similar meaning to the underlined word.

1 It's my <u>duty</u> to show tourists around this art museum.

    a. dream   *b.* job   *c.* hobby   *d.* happiness

2 They thought of ways of <u>getting around</u> the strict rules.

    a. reforming   *b.* creating   *c.* avoiding   *d.* following

C Choose the best word to complete each sentence.

1 You have to pay a fine. It is _____ to copy this DVD without permission.

    a. illegal   *b.* helpful   *c.* available   *d.* normal

2 I will not _____ you if you do the same thing again.

    a. establish   *b.* gain   *c.* forgive   *d.* represent

3 The terrible storm _____ many tall trees in my town.

    a. consisted of   *b.* came along   *c.* looked after   *d.* knocked down

4 The _____ leaders set up an organization to help the homeless.

    a. difficult   *b.* expensive   *c.* delicious   *d.* religious

Before Reading
If you could make your own perfume, which scent would you use?

Follow Your Nose!

Breathe in the scent of perfume through your nose, and let the feeling spread through your body. This is what I do as a perfumer. I fell in love with the magical power of perfume. That's why I became a perfumer.

Perfumers make beautiful perfumes by mixing various scents. We
5 know thousands of scents, such as the fresh smell of *citrus and the woody scent of a forest. And we have to be able to recognize each of these scents whether alone or mixed. So, only people with a delicate sense of smell can become perfumers. This is why we are sometimes called "noses."

Making perfume is an art. Like other artists, we turn a certain feeling
10 or image into a creation — in this case, a perfume. _____(A)_____, for a concept like "passion," we first make a new "recipe." This recipe is the list of different scents that match the image of "passion" and their amounts. We then mix them several times, changing the quantity of each ingredient of fragrance each time. We keep changing the recipe until we get the scent
15 just right. This process can take months or even years!

As you can see, making perfumes is an attractive job, but it requires years of training. Nowadays some people even take university-level courses to become perfumers. But the most important thing that one must absolutely have is a love for perfume!

*citrus: a type of juicy fruit that includes oranges and lemons

40

1 What is the best title for the passage?

   a. Create Your Own Recipes!

   b. How to Choose a Proper Perfume

   c. Creating the Most Beautiful Aromas

   d. Advantages of Taking University Courses

2 Why are perfumers sometimes called "noses"? (Choose two.)

   a. Because they know many different scents.

   b. Because they can smell anything from a distance.

   c. Because they have bigger noses than other people.

   d. Because they can distinguish each scent in a mix of scents.

3 The writer compares perfumers to artists because

_____ .

4 What is the best choice for blank (A)?

   a. Moreover   *b.* Therefore

   c. For example   *d.* On the other hand

5 What is most important for someone who wants to be a perfumer?

   a. Years of training

   b. A university education

   c. A passion for fragrance

   d. The creativity of an artist

6 What is NOT mentioned about perfumers?

   a. Where they get the ingredients for perfumes

   b. What they do when making a new perfume

   c. How long they spend making new recipes

   d. What is required to become one

Fill in the blanks with the correct words.

Perfumers

What a perfumer does
- Creates a perfume to describe a certain feeling or _____

How a perfumer makes a new perfume
- By mixing the perfect kinds of _____ in the right amounts to match a chosen concept

What is required to become a perfumer
- A delicate _____ of smell
- Lots of training and a(n) _____ for fragrance

| sense | image | quantity | love | scents |

★ EXPANDING KNOWLEDGE ★

English Dictionary   **smell**   ▼   **Search**

| *Related Search* | nerve | sight | hearing | touch | taste |
| | perceive | see | sound | feel | detect |

Synonyms
(good) • scent   • fragrance   • perfume
(bad)   • odor   • stink   • stench

Collocations
• a sense of smell   • a pleasant smell   • a disgusting smell   • a faint smell

Write the correct highlighted word next to its definition.

1 not strong or clear: _____

2 extremely unpleasant: _____

3 to notice or become aware of something: _____

4 a particular smell, especially an unpleasant one: _____

VOCABULARY REVIEW

A Write the correct word next to its definition.

attractive	fragrance	recipe	woody	passion

1 a pleasant smell: _____

2 having qualities that cause interest or desire: _____

3 a very strong belief or emotion about something: _____

4 a set of instructions telling you how to cook a certain dish: _____

B Find the word that has a similar meaning to the underlined word.

1 Building a house <u>requires</u> a lot of time and hard work.

   a. needs   *b.* saves   *c.* wastes   *d.* continues

2 I hadn't seen him for 10 years, so I didn't <u>recognize</u> him immediately.

   a. include   *b.* train   *c.* judge   *d.* identify

C Choose the best word to complete each sentence.

1 The _____ of her perfume was sweet and fresh.

   a. danger   *b.* noise   *c.* scent   *d.* invitation

2 Brown sugar is an important _____ in these cookies.

   a. skill   *b.* quantity   *c.* creation   *d.* ingredient

3 The police _____ the smell of alcohol in the room.

   a. abandoned   *b.* dropped   *c.* detected   *d.* celebrated

4 She can't see anything because she has lost her sense of _____.

   a. taste   *b.* sight   *c.* hearing   *d.* touch

Botox

Poisons are all around us. We can find them in plants, animals, and even in some kinds of food! They can cause serious harm, and some can even kill living things. However, there is a poison that gives us _____(A)_____. This is botulinum, also known as Botox. It is also called a "sausage poison,"
5 because it was first found in spoiled sausages.

Even though its nickname sounds strange, botulinum is one of the most fatal toxins in the world. It is so poisonous that just one gram of it can kill one million people! Once it enters the human body, it gradually paralyzes the muscles throughout the whole body. It starts with the muscles of the
10 face and then spreads to the arms and legs. People can die when it finally stops the muscles used for breathing from working.

Although botulinum is extremely dangerous, scientists found that it could be a helpful medicine for certain diseases. They discovered that if it is used in very small doses, it can prevent muscles from contracting! So this
15 fatal poison became a medicine to treat muscle disease. (①) But it has another special effect. (②) In 1987, a Canadian eye doctor used it to treat a patient with muscle problems around the eyes. (③) Since then, Botox has become more popular in cosmetic treatments. (④) A poison that threatens people's lives can sometimes help us!

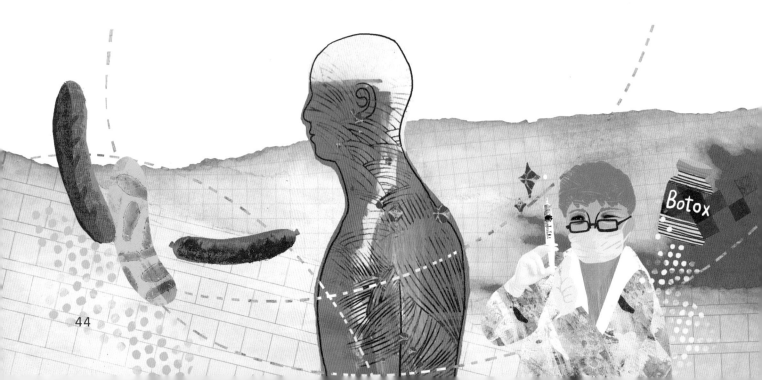

1 What is the best title for the passage?

    a. A Variety of Poisons around Us

    b. How to Prevent Food Poisoning

    c. A Great Cure from a Deadly Poison

    d. The Only Treatment for Muscle Disease

2 What is the best choice for blank (A)?

    a. mental damage

    b. pleasant feelings

    c. a terrible disaster

    d. unexpected benefits

3 Why is botulinum also called a "sausage poison"?

_____

4 What is the 2nd paragraph mainly about?

    a. Why we should avoid using Botox

    b. How the toxin affects the human body

    c. How many people have died from poisoning

    d. How long people have used Botox as a medicine

5 Where would the following sentence best fit?

> The doctor was surprised to find that it not only cured the problems, but also reduced facial wrinkles!

    a. ①   *b.* ②   *c.* ③   *d.* ④

6 Write T if the statement is true or F if it's false.

    1) Botulinum affects the human body from head to toe.

    2) Botox was originally developed as a treatment to reduce wrinkles.

Fill in the blanks with the correct words.

Botox

- First found in _____ that had gone bad
- Could kill one million people with only one gram of it
- _____ muscles from the face to the arms and legs
- Can treat muscle problems with a very small _____
- Also reduces _____ lines and wrinkles

| facial | poison | amount | sausages | paralyzes |

★ EXPANDING KNOWLEDGE ★

Did you know that some toxins that come from animals can be good for your health? The Chilean rose *tarantula's weak venom isn't much use to the spider, but it can help humans a lot. It contains a protein that can be used to stop heart attacks. Scorpions, meanwhile, produce a venom that can be mixed with other natural substances to make a medicine to treat cancer. The new treatment is so promising that the Cuban government has created large farms to breed thousands of scorpions. So don't be scared of large hairy spiders or scorpions. They could save your life some day!

*tarantula: a large spider covered with hair

1 What is the passage mainly about?

   a. Using toxins to kill harmful insects
   b. Why we should protect spiders and scorpions
   c. How to treat cancer with medicine from nature
   d. The health benefits of toxins from certain animals

2 Write T if the statement is true or F if it's false.

   1) The Chilean rose tarantula's venom causes people to have heart attacks.
   2) The Cuban government is raising scorpions to use their venom as medicine.

A Write the correct word next to its definition.

toxin	wrinkle	paralyze	contract	treatment

1 to become smaller or shorter: _____

2 the process of curing someone by using medicine: _____

3 to make someone unable to feel or move his or her body: _____

4 a small line on your skin that you get when you grow old: _____

B Find the word that has a similar meaning to the underlined word.

1 I was very sorry to hear that Chris has a <u>fatal</u> disease.

    a. rare   *b.* minor   *c.* deadly   *d.* common

2 His math grades have <u>gradually</u> improved for two years.

    a. slowly   *b.* suddenly   *c.* accidentally   *d.* surprisingly

C Choose the best word to complete each sentence.

1 Sally was impressed by the _____ surprise party.

    a. boring   *b.* advanced   *c.* unexpected   *d.* disappointing

2 Terrorist groups that _____ world peace are a big problem.

    a. cure   *b.* seek   *c.* praise   *d.* threaten

3 You should be extra careful when you're handling this _____ chemical.

    a. gentle   *b.* safe   *c.* hairy   *d.* poisonous

4 When I mentioned the man's name, Betty changed her _____ expression.

    a. blind   *b.* facial   *c.* narrow   *d.* harmful

Before Reading
What kind of discomfort have you experienced on planes?

Flight Fee for the Obese

Some airlines have considered charging obese passengers more than others. They would have to buy two seats if they can't fit into
5 *one. Some students are debating this issue.*

Robert: I think every passenger has the right to have a comfortable trip. And when extremely large people sit next to you, you have to share your seat, which can be uncomfortable. I heard that some airlines
10 in America received hundreds of discomfort complaints for this reason. Airlines have to do something to fix this problem!

Sophie: Airlines don't care about obese customers. This is not how companies are supposed to act. _____(A)_____ charging them more, airlines could make an effort to offer them bigger seats!
15 Disneyland in California, for instance, made their ride seats bigger to fit the needs of their larger customers. Airlines should learn from them.

Cathy: As a business, an airline must consider high gas prices. The heavier the plane is, the more gas it uses. ① That's why they charge more
20 for excess baggage. ② But weight for excess baggage varies among airlines. ③ So why not for people? ④ If a person weighs so much that the airline must pay more for gas, then that customer should share the burden!

Daniel: I don't think human beings should be compared to baggage.
25 Charging them more for being too fat is rude and offensive. What's more, in many cases being obese isn't a matter of choice. Many obese people aren't overweight simply because of a lack of self-control when it comes to food. Obesity is a serious medical condition. These people need extra care, not another embarrassing situation.

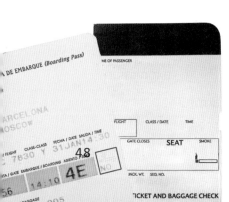

1 Who supports charging obese passengers more money? (Choose two.)

    a. Robert   *b.* Sophie   *c.* Cathy   *d.* Daniel

2 What is the best choice for blank (A)?

    a. Instead of

    b. In spite of

    c. Because of

    d. As a result of

3 What does Sophie say airlines should learn from Disneyland?

    a. How to increase profits

    b. How to satisfy customers

    c. How to avoid obese customers

    d. How to make new facilities safer

4 Which sentence is not needed in the passage?

    a. ①   *b.* ②   *c.* ③   *d.* ④

5 According to Daniel, why do obese passengers need extra care?

6 Who agrees with the following idea?

> It is reasonable that airline companies follow economic principles.

    a. Robert   *b.* Sophie   *c.* Cathy   *d.* Daniel

Fill in the blanks with the correct words.

Charging Obese Passengers More Money

Pros
- Robert: Sitting next to obese passengers causes _____.
  Many people complain about this.
- Cathy: The heavier the plane is, the more gas it uses.
  Obese people have to _____ the costs of gas.

Cons
- Sophie: Airlines should _____ about obese passengers.
  They should provide bigger seats for them.
- Daniel: It's rude and _____ to obese people.
  Obesity is a serious medical condition, so these people need
  more attention.

| offensive | poor | discomfort | share | care |

★ EXPANDING KNOWLEDGE ★

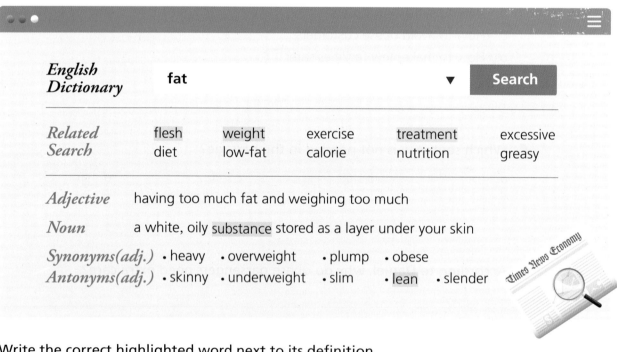

English Dictionary	fat				▼	**Search**

Related Search	flesh	weight	exercise	treatment	excessive
	diet	low-fat	calorie	nutrition	greasy

Adjective	having too much fat and weighing too much
Noun	a white, oily substance stored as a layer under your skin
Synonyms(adj.)	• heavy • overweight • plump • obese
Antonyms(adj.)	• skinny • underweight • slim • lean • slender

Write the correct highlighted word next to its definition.

1 a particular type of material: _____

2 having very little fat but looking healthy: _____

3 the soft part of the body between the skin and bones: _____

4 a measurement of how heavy someone or something is: _____

Unit 11
VOCABULARY REVIEW

A Write the correct word next to its definition.

offensive	vary	debate	charge	excess

1 more than the amount that is necessary: _____

2 to require an amount of money for a service: _____

3 to argue about a subject in a formal manner: _____

4 very insulting and likely to upset other people: _____

B Find the word that has a similar meaning to the underlined word.

1 He managed to <u>fix</u> the problem on his own.

a. solve   b. cause   c. attach   d. prepare

2 This parking lot can only be used by <u>customers</u> at our department store.

a. owners   b. vehicles   c. tourists   d. consumers

C Choose the best word to complete each sentence.

1 The new tablet PC is small enough to _____ in your pocket.

a. fit   b. weigh   c. compare   d. purchase

2 Jeff made a _____ about the poor service in the store.

a. trip   b. praise   c. direction   d. complaint

3 It is very _____ of you to say such a hurtful thing.

a. rude   b. timid   c. nice   d. independent

4 The interviewer asked me _____ questions that I didn't know how to answer.

a. easy   b. amusing   c. pleasant   d. embarrassing

Voytek

Did you know that a brave bear played an important role in the Second World War? This is the story of the soldier bear named Voytek.

The story begins in 1942, when Polish soldiers in Iran found a tiny bear. (①) Having lost his mother, the bear thought of the soldiers as his parents. (②) He cried when he was lonely and covered his eyes with his paws when someone shouted at him. (③) He also loved drinking beer, smoking cigarettes, and wrestling with the soldiers. (④)

The bear was so popular with the Polish soldiers that he became their mascot. As he got older, he started _____(A)_____. He carried heavy bombs

15 and huge boxes of bullets, which a man could never do alone. Once he even discovered an enemy spy! When the soldiers were sent to Italy in 1944, they wanted to take him with them. But the only way to do that was to enlist him in the Polish army. So they gave him a name, rank, and number. His name, "Voytek," means "he

20 who enjoys war" or "smiling warrior."

After the war, Voytek retired to the Edinburgh Zoo in Scotland. Former Polish soldiers sometimes visited and threw cigarettes to him. They said he could still understand the Polish language. Voytek died in 1963, but he will never

25 be forgotten. There are sculptures and signs in Edinburgh, London, and Ottawa in memory of Voytek.

1 What is the best title for the passage?

   a. The First Humanlike Bear
   b. Voytek: The Brave Soldier Bear
   c. The High Intelligence of Wild Bears
   d. The Tragedy of the Second World War

2 Where would the following sentence best fit?

As a result, he started acting like a human.

   a. ①   b. ②   c. ③   d. ④

3 What can be inferred from the 2nd paragraph?

   a. Wild bears were commonly found in Iran in the past.
   b. Polish soldiers were allowed to have pets during the war.
   c. The Polish soldiers took care of Voytek instead of his mother.
   d. Animals were trained to attack enemy soldiers during WW II.

4 What is the best choice for blank (A)?

   a. working as a spy
   b. making weapons
   c. helping the soldiers
   d. traveling around the world

5 What did Polish soldiers have to do to take Voytek to Italy?

   _____

6 What is NOT true about Voytek?

   a. He was greatly loved by his fellow soldiers.
   b. He died during the Second World War.
   c. He lived for more than 20 years.
   d. He is still remembered in many places.

Fill in the blanks with the correct words.

During World War II, a young bear was found and _____ by Polish soldiers. He acted like a human and became the soldiers' _____. As he grew, he even learned to help the soldiers in battle. They liked him so much that they _____ him in the Polish army to take him to Italy. After the war, the bear was taken to a zoo in Edinburgh. Polish soldiers visited him until his death, and even today he is _____ around the world.

mascot	enlisted	raised	retired	remembered

★ EXPANDING KNOWLEDGE ★

Encyclopedia Contents: World War II

1. Date: September 1, 1939–September 2, 1945
2. Background
   2.1 Aftermath of WW I
   2.2 Rise of nationalism
   2.3 Fascism in Italy
   2.4 Nazism in Germany
3. Pre-war events
   3.1 Italian invasion of Ethiopia (1935)
   3.2 Spanish Civil War (1936–39)
   3.3 Japanese invasion of China (1937)
4. Course of the war
   4.1 War breaks out in Europe (1939–40)
   4.2 Axis attacks the Soviet Union (1941)
   4.3 Pacific War breaks out (1941)
   4.4 Axis advance stops (1942–43)
   4.5 Allies gain momentum (1943–44)
   4.6 Axis collapses, Allies win (1944–45)
5. Impact
   5.1 Casualties and war crimes
   5.2 Concentration camps, slave labor, and genocide

1 Write the correct highlighted word next to its definition.

1) the murder of a whole group of people: _____

2) the situation that explains why something happens: _____

3) the act of an army entering another country by force: _____

2 Write T if the statement is true or F if it's false.

1) The Second World War lasted for 6 years.

2) At the end of the war, the Axis made peace with the Allies.

Unit·12
VOCABULARY REVIEW

A Write the correct word next to its definition.

| paw | bullet | mascot | soldier | sculpture |

1 a person who is in an army: _____

2 the clawed foot of an animal: _____

3 a small piece of metal that is fired from a gun: _____

4 an object made by carving or shaping stone, wood, clay, etc.: _____

B Find the word that has the opposite meaning of the underlined word.

1 The war has killed more than 5,000 people since it broke out.

   a. ended   *b.* began   *c.* lasted   *d.* approached

2 Don't forget to change the password to your account regularly.

   a. leave   *b.* recall   *c.* choose   *d.* neglect

C Choose the best word to complete each sentence.

1 He decided to _____ from his position because of his poor health.

   a. hire   *b.* work   *c.* start   *d.* retire

2 He founded a hospital in _____ of his late wife.

   a. case   *b.* moment   *c.* memory   *d.* search

3 Someone was trying to steal my bag, so I _____ for help.

   a. carried   *b.* shouted   *c.* refused   *d.* produced

4 Light plays an important _____ in the growth of plants.

   a. role   *b.* hole   *c.* region   *d.* nutrient

Cirque du Soleil

Colorful spotlights hit the stage; merry music starts playing; acrobats in beautiful clothes cheerfully dance onto the stage — the show has begun! You've stepped out of reality and entered the magical world of *Cirque du Soleil*. This world-famous entertainment company founded in 1984 by
5 two Canadian street performers has completely changed the art of circus performance.

So what are *Cirque du Soleil*'s unique features? It doesn't have clowns making silly jokes or animals jumping through hoops. Instead, it combines classic circus acts with various other artistic elements, such as drama, dance,
10 live music, and even a fashion show. Gymnastics is also mixed in, with acrobats performing unbelievable tricks. In order to put on such amazing shows, *Cirque* searches for the best performers in the world, including Olympic athletes!

But more importantly, each performance _____(A)_____. For example, "*Quidam," one of *Cirque*'s most famous shows, is about a girl named Zoe. ① She is bored and trying to get her parents' attention. ② Actually, many people sometimes feel bored during the performance. ③ Then one day, a man called Quidam visits her and drops his hat. ④ When she puts on the hat, her boring world is changed into a colorful and lively one.

Currently, *Cirque du Soleil* shows are being performed in every corner of the world. About 90 million people in more than 200 cities have experienced the magic of these performances. Don't miss your chance to see one of these amazing shows when *Cirque* comes to your city!

*Quidam: "a nameless passerby" in Latin

1 What is the best title for the passage?

　　a. The World's Most Fantastic Circus
　　b. The Popularity of Traditional Circuses
　　c. Great Athletes in the Olympic Games
　　d. Change Your Boring World with Quidam

2 When and by whom was *Cirque du Soleil* founded?

　　_____

3 What is NOT mentioned as a unique feature of *Cirque du Soleil*?

　　a. It doesn't show any clowns or jumping animals.
　　b. It features many different forms of entertainment.
　　c. It has a magic show that involves unbelievable tricks.
　　d. It hires the most talented performers in the world.

4 What is the best choice for blank (A)?

　　a. has an interesting story
　　b. attracts a large audience
　　c. uses expensive stage equipment
　　d. spends lots of money on advertising

5 Which sentence is NOT needed in the passage?

　　a. ①　　　　　b. ②　　　　　c. ③　　　　　d. ④

6 Write T if the statement is true or F if it's false.

　　1) *Cirque du Soleil* performances never use traditional circus acts.
　　2) People of many countries can see a *Cirque du Soleil* show, as it travels around the world.

Fill in the blanks with the correct words.

Cirque du Soleil

- Founded by two Canadian street performers in 1984

- Mixes many different _____ elements with classic circus acts
- Performed by the most _____ performers in the world
- Includes an interesting _____ in each performance

- Has become _____ and is performed in many countries

> world-famous   traditional   story   talented   artistic

★ EXPANDING KNOWLEDGE ★

When I was in Las Vegas, I saw a *Cirque du Soleil* show called "O." It was an aquatic show, and its name "O" comes from "eau," the French word for _____(A)_____. The first thing we saw in the theater was a big pool. The show was about a magical fantasy world both inside and outside of the pool. Synchronized swimmers started the show, and various other characters appeared after. My favorite character was the Masked Thief, who played with fire! I also liked the music, which featured the sounds of many unique instruments, like African guitars and Chinese violins. I loved the show so much that I want to watch it again!

1 What is the best choice for blank (A)?

 a. air   *b.* fire

 c. water   *d.* universe

2 Write T if the statement is true or F if it's false.

 1) The name of the show, "O," comes from a French word.

 2) The Masked Thief, one of the main characters, played with water.

Unit · 13
VOCABULARY REVIEW

A Write the correct word next to its definition.

trick	attention	aquatic	performance	clown

1 living in or related to water: _____

2 special care, action, or treatment for someone or something: _____

3 the action of entertaining other people by dancing, singing, or acting: _____

4 a person who wears funny clothes and does silly things to amuse others: _____

B Find the word that has a similar meaning to the underlined word.

1 The most distinctive feature of Van Gogh's paintings is their bright colors.

    a. advancement   *b.* creature   *c.* future   *d.* characteristic

2 To cook the food, she combined eggs with a little flour.

    a. provided   *b.* divided   *c.* mixed   *d.* purchased

C Choose the best word to complete each sentence.

1 When his business failed, he wanted to escape from _____.

    a. dream   *b.* fantasy   *c.* hoop   *d.* reality

2 The police are _____ for proof that the criminal killed the woman.

    a. supporting   *b.* searching   *c.* jumping   *d.* hitting

3 It is very _____ of you to cry over such a thing.

    a. wise   *b.* silly   *c.* mature   *d.* patient

4 Tom is good at sports, so he wants to be a professional _____.

    a. surgeon   *b.* lawyer   *c.* performer   *d.* athlete

PSYCHOLOGY

Before Reading
What would you do if you saw a broken window in your neighbor's house?

Broken Windows Theory

Imagine you want to throw away some trash, but there is no trash can around. So you just throw it in a place where there is a lot of trash. It seems okay because the place is already quite messy. This is a case that shows how the "broken windows theory" works.

According to this theory, if a window in a building is broken and left unrepaired, the rest of the windows will soon be broken. This is because an unrepaired broken window makes the building look uncared for. This attracts people who want to break the other windows. To test this theory, a researcher did an experiment with an old car. He parked the car on a street, but nobody

15 touched it at first. However, after the researcher damaged the car, some other people came along and began to _____(A)_____!

This theory tells us that disorder can encourage bad behavior. Similarly, if we neglect minor crimes, they can lead to additional and more serious ones. By that point, it's too late to solve the problem by repairing the

20 original "broken window." For this reason, police forces in some cities, including New York, pay close attention to small crimes like littering and making graffiti. As a result, they have reduced the number of serious crimes. So you shouldn't ignore

25 small problems. If you do, they can lead to bigger, uncontrollable problems in the future!

1 What is the best title for the passage?

    a. A War against Crime and Violence

    b. The Need for Trash Cans in Dirty Places

    c. Broken Windows: Things You Shouldn't Touch

    d. Broken Windows Can Lead to Bigger Problems

2 How does the writer introduce the topic?

    a. By giving several crime theories

    b. By explaining the reasons for small crimes

    c. By telling why we should have more trash cans

    d. By giving an example of the broken windows theory

3 Why do people break more windows when they see an unrepaired one in a building?

4 What is the best choice for blank (A)?

    a. cause more damage

    b. report it to the police

    c. repair its broken parts

    d. ask about the research

5 What does the underlined sentence mean?

    a. The original broken window doesn't need to be repaired.

    b. It will take much more time and effort to solve the problem.

    c. It is hard to find the proper window to replace the broken one.

    d. Broken windows are dangerous, so we have to repair them right away.

6 Write T if the statement is true or F if it's false.

    1) In an experiment, the researcher parked a car that had already been damaged.

    2) New York City has reduced serious crimes by focusing on small ones.

STRATEGIC ORGANIZER

Fill in the blanks with the correct words.

Broken Windows Theory — If a broken window is left _____, all the other windows will soon be broken.

Experiment
• If a damaged car is parked, people begin to _____ it.

Effects in reality
• Minor crimes may lead to more _____ ones.
• Following this theory, police forces _____ small crimes.

attack   serious   changed   focus on   unrepaired

★ EXPANDING KNOWLEDGE ★

English Dictionary	crime			▼	**Search**

Related Search	arrest detective	criminal evidence	suspect judgment	victim guilty	illegal prison

Synonyms
• violation   • offense   • misdeed

Collocations
• a crime scene   • a crime rate   • a violent crime
• a political crime   • commit a crime   • confess one's crime
• witness a crime

Write the correct highlighted word next to its definition.

1 a decision made in a court: _____

2 not being allowed by the law: _____

3 someone who commits a crime: _____

4 someone who has been attacked or killed as a result of a crime: _____

VOCABULARY REVIEW

A Write the correct word next to its definition.

minor	crime	graffiti	behavior	encourage

1 an activity that is against the law: _____

2 small and less important or serious: _____

3 to make something happen or exist: _____

4 words or drawings on walls in public places: _____

B Find the word that has a similar meaning to the underlined word.

1 The company needs strategies to <u>attract</u> customers.

   a. draw   *b.* avoid   *c.* require   *d.* perform

2 The office is so <u>messy</u> that we should clean it right now.

   a. busy   *b.* dirty   *c.* direct   *d.* large

C Choose the best word to complete each sentence.

1 I believe that hard work will _____ success.

   a. solve   *b.* damage   *c.* neglect   *d.* lead to

2 I think we need _____ research to finish this report.

   a. difficult   *b.* unrepaired   *c.* expensive   *d.* additional

3 She _____ her headache, thinking it would pass soon.

   a. cured   *b.* caused   *c.* ignored   *d.* prevented

4 Because of the war, the whole country is in a state of _____.

   a. display   *b.* disorder   *c.* freedom   *d.* recovery

Gross National Happiness

Many people believe that the more things they have, the happier they will be. But is this true? The answer can be found in Bhutan.

① Bhutan is a tiny Himalayan Buddhist kingdom. ② It's one of the least developed countries in the world, and most of its people are very poor. ③ So people in Bhutan had to find refuge in religion. ④ But surprisingly, Bhutan is the eighth-happiest country in the world. How is this possible? It's because of a special standard they use for measuring the happiness of the people. It's called Gross National Happiness (GNH), and it was created by Bhutan's King Wangchuck in 1972. He believed material wealth doesn't necessarily bring happiness. So he decided to help his people in other ways, focusing on
15 their happiness instead of _____(A)_____.

To increase GNH, the government tries to improve people's health by providing free healthcare to everyone. If it's impossible to treat an illness in Bhutan, the government sends the patient to a hospital abroad. _____(B)_____, the government makes an effort to protect the country's
20 environment and culture. In order to do this, it carefully regulates tourism. Tourists can travel to Bhutan only through licensed Bhutanese tour operators and agents. Also, there's a law which says that 60 percent of
25 the country has to remain forested.

So whenever you feel unhappy because you think that you don't have much, remember Bhutan. Happiness doesn't depend
30 on money!

1 What is the best title for the passage?

    a. Be Rich As Soon As Possible

    b. Money Can't Buy Happiness

    c. The Unique Political System of Bhutan

    d. The Secret of Tourism's Success in Bhutan

2 Which sentence is NOT needed in the passage?

    a. ①   *b.* ②   *c.* ③   *d.* ④

3 What is the best choice for blank (A)?

    a. social duty

    b. economic value

    c. cultural heritage

    d. educational standards

4 What is the best choice for blank (B)?

    a. However   *b.* Therefore

    c. In addition   *d.* For example

5 What is NOT mentioned as a policy of the Bhutanese government?

    a. To give people healthcare without demanding any money

    b. To send some patients abroad to foreign hospitals

    c. To prevent tourists from visiting Bhutan

    d. To protect a percentage of forests in the country

6 Write T if the statement is true or F if it's false.

    1) Though Bhutan is a poor country, most of its people are satisfied with their lives.

    2) Bhutan's king thought that material things are closely related to happiness.

STRATEGIC SUMMARY

Fill in the blanks with the correct words.

Bhutan is a country which proves that money can't buy _____.
Even though most of its people are very _____, they're also
some of the happiest people in the world. This is because of the concept
of Gross National Happiness developed by a king of Bhutan. This index
_____ how happy a nation's people are. In order to keep the
people happy, the Bhutanese government works to _____ public
services, such as healthcare, while protecting the culture and environment
of the country.

wealth	measures	improve	happiness	poor

★ EXPANDING KNOWLEDGE ★

Encyclopedia Contents: Happiness

1. Definition: an emotional state of well-being

2. Factors influencing happiness
   2.1 Health
   2.2 Social interaction
   2.3 Accomplishments
   2.4 Wealth
   2.5 Religion

3. Measurement of happiness
   3.1 SHS (Subjective Happiness Scale)
   3.2 PANAS (Positive and Negative Affect Schedule)
   3.3 SWLS (Satisfaction with Life Scale)
   3.4 GNH (Gross National Happiness)

1 Write the correct highlighted word next to its definition.

1) the belief in and worship of a god or gods: _____

2) the activity of talking or doing things with other people: _____

3) the pleasure that you get when achieving what you want: _____

2 Write T if the statement is true or F if it's false.

1) People are naturally likely to feel happy, regardless of how healthy they are.

2) Not having enough money may affect one's level of happiness.

VOCABULARY REVIEW

A Write the correct word next to its definition.

create	kingdom	wealth	tourism	Buddhist

1 a country ruled by a king or queen: _____

2 a large amount of money that a person has: _____

3 to make something exist that did not exist before: _____

4 the business of providing services to people on vacation: _____

B Find the word that has a similar meaning to the underlined word.

1 Clare remained silent while all her friends were having an exciting conversation.

   a. grew   *b.* proved   *c.* stayed   *d.* seemed

2 She is treating her depression with laughter therapy.

   a. hiding   *b.* forgetting   *c.* making   *d.* curing

C Choose the best word to complete each sentence.

1 Kids stood against a wall and drew a line to _____ their own height.

   a. increase   *b.* maintain   *c.* measure   *d.* reduce

2 I started taking private lessons to _____ my grades.

   a. give   *b.* improve   *c.* confuse   *d.* worsen

3 The fire caused a lot of _____ damage.

   a. material   *b.* innovative   *c.* effective   *d.* innocent

4 We should _____ smoking in public places to protect people's health.

   a. suggest   *b.* recommend   *c.* regulate   *d.* propose

Winchester House

In California, there is an enormous mansion called the Winchester House. It looks like just a beautiful house, but actually it is considered haunted.

It was built by Sarah Winchester in 1884. Her husband William owned a rifle manufacturing company. (①) She lived a happy life before her husband and daughter died suddenly from diseases. (②)

While suffering from sadness, she was told by a famous *psychic that her troubles were caused by the spirits of those who were shot dead by her husband's guns. (③) So she started building a home for these spirits, and she worked on the house every day for the next 38 years. (④)

10   The house has many strange features. _____(A)_____, it has 160 rooms and about 10,000 windows. Many staircases lead to a ceiling or wall, and there are dozens of secret passageways. One staircase has 44 steps but rises only about 2 meters, since each step is just 5 centimeters high. There are several possible reasons for these features. Some say Mrs. Winchester

15 wanted to confuse evil spirits, so she made the house complicated. Others say because of her severe arthritis, the house was designed to help her feel less pain. Whether or not either of these is true, there were no plans to follow or inspections made during the house's construction, so it

20 turned out very unusual.

Nowadays people from around the world come and see the house. If you want to visit it, be careful. Without a tour guide, you

25 may never find your way out!

*psychic: a person who claims to have mysterious mental powers

1 What is the best title for the passage?

    a. The Tragic Life of Mrs. Winchester

    b. Winchester House: The Mysterious Mansion

    c. An Effective Way of Escaping from Evil Spirits

    d. Winchester House: An Architect's Greatest Work

2 According to the psychic, what caused Mrs. Winchester's troubles?

_____

3 Where would the following sentence best fit?

> The psychic told her she must build a house and keep building it
> without stopping.

    a. ①   *b.* ②   *c.* ③   *d.* ④

4 What is the best choice for blank (A)?

    a. Finally   *b.* However

    c. As a result   *d.* For example

5 What is NOT mentioned as a reason for the strange features of the Winchester House?

    a. Mrs. Winchester wanted to confuse evil spirits.

    b. It was designed to relieve the pain she felt from a disease.

    c. It was constructed without planning or supervision.

    d. Mrs. Winchester wanted to make her house unique and popular.

6 Write T if the statement is true or F if it's false.

    1) The husband of Mrs. Winchester died because of a gun accident.

    2) The Winchester House was under construction for almost 40 years.

Fill in the blanks with the correct words.

The Winchester House in California looks like just a beautiful house, but it is considered _____ . Sarah Winchester built the house shortly after her husband and daughter died. Sarah was told that spirits from the dead were causing her _____ , so she decided to build a house for the spirits. The house has many _____ passages and stairs that end at walls or the ceiling. Some say the strange house was built to _____ the spirits, while others say it was built to help Sarah manage her arthritis. Today, the house has become a world-famous tourist attraction.

> secret   haunted   troubles   confuse   construction

★ EXPANDING KNOWLEDGE ★

English Dictionary	spirit				▼	**Search**

Related Search	horrifying	illusion	scary	mystery	superstition
	devil	angel	soul	ghost	

Noun

1. [uncountable] the part of a person that includes the mind and feelings rather than the body (= soul)
   I believe in the power of the human spirit.
2. [countable] a supernatural being (= ghost)
   I can still feel my grandfather's spirit in this house.

Collocations
- an evil spirit
- a restless spirit
- the spirits of the dead

Write the correct highlighted word next to its definition.

1 connected with the forces of the devil: _____

2 not possible to explain by natural laws: _____

3 the spiritual part of a human being separate from the body: _____

4 something that seems real but is actually false or doesn't exist: _____

Unit · 16
VOCABULARY REVIEW

A Write the correct word next to its definition.

severe	haunted	horrifying	rifle	secret

1 very bad or serious: _____

2 visited regularly by a ghost: _____

3 very shocking or frightening: _____

4 kept hidden from other people: _____

B Find the word that has a similar meaning to the underlined word.

1 The <u>enormous</u> house will be built right beside the lake.

    a. red   *b.* new   *c.* huge   *d.* wooden

2 This machine is more <u>complicated</u> than I thought.

    a. easy   *b.* boring   *c.* complex   *d.* convenient

C Choose the best word to complete each sentence.

1 It was _____ being all alone in a dark room.

    a. sour   *b.* scary   *c.* rough   *d.* violent

2 He is so rich that he _____ several building and houses.

    a. suffers   *b.* suggests   *c.* brings   *d.* owns

3 That beautiful _____ was built in the 1950s.

    a. planet   *b.* height   *c.* mansion   *d.* countryside

4 My wife died of cancer, but I think her _____ is always with me.

    a. path   *b.* spirit   *c.* inventor   *d.* character

TECHNOLOGY

Brain-Computer Interface

Have you seen the movie *Minority Report*? In it, there is a scene where a computer senses a human's brainwaves. Then it shows what the person is thinking on a screen. You may think that this is just a fantasy. But it is actually not so unrealistic, because there is now technology that can read
5 people's brainwaves!

The technology is called a brain-computer interface, or BCI. (①) It is a way of connecting a person's brain to a computer. (②) For this system to work, scientists attach a special chip to a person's brain. (③) Then the computer interprets the meaning of the signals and tells a device what
10 to do. (④) In this way, the person can control the device with his or her thoughts. Using BCI, people can already write letters or play computer games. Now scientists are working on ways for people to operate television sets and cellphones just by thinking.

However, this technology is not drawing attention just because it is
15 convenient and fun. In addition, it _____(A)_____. For example, a robotic arm or leg can be attached to a person's body. Then, using BCI, the person thinks about moving it, over and over again. Eventually, the robotic device "learns" to move when its owner wants it to. In the future, this may allow paralyzed people to walk on their own!

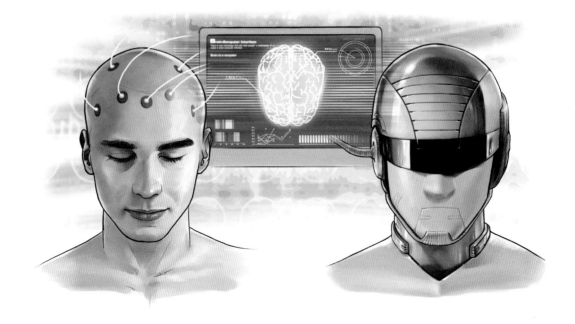

1 What is the best title for the passage?

    a. Mind Reading Technology

    b. Advanced Special Effects in Movies

    c. How to Play Computer Games Well

    d. The Convenience of Automatic Machines

2 Why does the writer mention the movie *Minority Report*?

    a. To explain how interesting the movie is

    b. To emphasize how unrealistic BCI technology is

    c. To describe what special effects are used in movies

    d. To introduce technology that reads people's brainwaves

3 Where would the following sentence best fit?

> This chip detects brain signals and sends them to a computer.

    a. ①   *b.* ②   *c.* ③   *d.* ④

4 What are scientists working on now that involves BCI?

_____

5 What is the best choice for blank (A)?

    a. can cure serious diseases

    b. gives hope to the disabled

    c. makes people disappointed

    d. is something useless and old-fashioned

6 Write T if the statement is true or F if it's false.

    1) BCI attracts attention mostly because of its entertainment value.

    2) By using BCI, the disabled may be able to walk by themselves in the future.

Fill in the blanks with the correct words.

A brain-computer interface (BCI) is technology that makes it possible to control electronic devices simply by _____. This is done by _____ a special chip to a person's brain. This chip sends brain signals to a computer, and the computer reads the meaning of the person's brainwaves and tells the device what to do. BCI has many possible fun and _____ uses. For example, it can be used to play video games and operate a cellphone. But more importantly, it may allow _____ people to lead normal lives thanks to mind-controlled robotic arms and legs.

> convenient　　thinking　　paralyzed　　controlling　　attaching

★ EXPANDING KNOWLEDGE ★

Encyclopedia Contents: Human Brain

1. Structure
  1.1 Divisions: four sections
  1.2 Skull: brain protection
2. Functions
  2.1 Information processing
  2.2 Perception
  2.3 Body movement control
  2.4 Learning and memory
  2.5 Language
  2.6 Metabolism

3. Brain damage and diseases
  3.1 Stroke
  3.2 Brain tumor
  3.3 Alzheimer's disease
  3.4 Parkinson's syndrome
  3.5 Mental diseases

1 Write the correct highlighted word next to its definition.

1) to deal with information: _____

2) the act of keeping someone or something safe: _____

3) the ability to become aware of something through senses: _____

2 Write T if the statement is true or F if it's false.

1) The human brain is divided into four parts.

2) Mental illness has nothing to do with brain damage.

Unit 17
VOCABULARY REVIEW

A Write the correct word next to its definition.

meaning	attach	device	convenient	automatic

1 working by itself: _____

2 useful or easy to use: _____

3 to join or connect one thing to another: _____

4 a machine or tool that was designed to do a special job: _____

B Find the word that has a similar meaning to the underlined word.

1 The brand-new blender is very easy to operate.

   a. fix   *b.* use   *c.* sell   *d.* clean

2 A fire alarm senses smoke from fires.

   a. blows   *b.* stops   *c.* detects   *d.* protects

C Choose the best word to complete each sentence.

1 The sinking ship sent out an emergency _____.

   a. condition   *b.* scene   *c.* signal   *d.* screen

2 The dream you have is too _____. It will never happen!

   a. calm   *b.* polite   *c.* attractive   *d.* unrealistic

3 The same situation can be _____ differently depending on one's view.

   a. interviewed   *b.* interpreted   *c.* interacted   *d.* interrupted

4 The pilot couldn't _____ the airplane, and it crashed into the sea.

   a. admire   *b.* compete   *c.* control   *d.* connect

Light Pollution

Have you ever been in the countryside and looked up at the stars? They look amazing! But in the city, you probably can't see any stars. Why is that? It is the bright lights that make it hard for us

5　to see stars. This problem is called light pollution. It is caused by things like street lights, neon signs, and the lights in our homes.

　　But not seeing the stars is not the only problem. Light pollution causes serious health problems, too. It has even been linked to breast cancer. According to scientists, light pollution stops our bodies from producing

10　enough melatonin, an important chemical that fights breast cancer. Light pollution also prevents some people from sleeping normally and gives others higher blood pressure.

　　Light pollution is also bad for _____(A)_____. All living things depend on the natural balance of light and dark. ① Too much artificial light can

15　hinder plants' growth and threaten their lives. ② When a flower dies, a fruit begins to grow. ③ In addition, extra light can confuse animals, especially those that are active at night. ④ It also affects their ability to breed.

　　So, what is being done to solve this problem? The International Dark-Sky Association (IDA) has encouraged governments to change laws about

20　lighting and introduce better lighting systems. As a result, many cities in Italy have changed their street lamps to prevent light from escaping sideways and upwards. If more places make an effort like that, we'll all be able to see beautiful stars again!

1 What is the best title for the passage?

　　a. Tips for Preventing Light Pollution

　　b. An Amazing Beauty: Night Views of Cities

　　c. Turn Off the Lights for Yourself and Nature

　　d. The Relationship between Melatonin and Breast Cancer

2 What does the underlined sentence mean?

　　a. Not seeing the stars is not a problem at all.

　　b. There are no problems except not seeing the stars.

　　c. Not seeing the stars can cause many other problems.

　　d. There are also other problems caused by light pollution.

3 What is the best choice for blank (A)?

　　a. farming

　　b. the environment

　　c. natural resources

　　d. the local economy

4 Which sentence is NOT needed in the passage?

　　a. ①　　　　　　*b.* ②　　　　　　*c.* ③　　　　　　*d.* ④

5 What has IDA done to solve the problem of light pollution?

6 Write T if the statement is true or F if it's false.

　　1) A person who has less melatonin is more likely to get breast cancer.

　　2) All animals need lots of light to be active and to breed.

Fill in the blanks with the correct words.

Light Pollution

Causes
• _____ lights in cities

Effects on health
• Increases _____ of breast cancer
• Disturbs normal _____ patterns and raises blood pressure

Effects on the environment
• Causes _____ not to grow well, even to die
• Confuses animals that are active at night and affects their breeding

| risk | plants | bright | sleeping | chemical |

★ EXPANDING KNOWLEDGE ★

Encyclopedia Contents: Pollution

1. Types and causes
   1.1 Air pollution
      1.1.1 Fossil fuels, car emissions
   1.2 Water pollution
      1.2.1 Wastewater, natural disaster
   1.3 Light pollution
      1.3.1 Excessive lighting
   1.4 Soil pollution
      1.4.1 Pesticides, littering

2. Effects
   2.1 Human health
   2.2 Environment
3. Movements
   3.1 Individuals
      3.1.2 3Rs: reduce, reuse, recycle
   3.2 Nations
      3.2.1 Kyoto Protocol: control of
            greenhouse gas emissions

1 Write the correct highlighted word next to its definition.

1) something that causes great damage: _____

2) a gas or other substance released into the air: _____

3) an arrangement or plan made between countries: _____

2 Write T if the statement is true or F if it's false.

1) Burning coal and using cars can cause air to be more polluted.

2) The Kyoto Protocol was intended to prevent water from being polluted.

Unit 18
VOCABULARY REVIEW

A Write the correct word next to its definition.

| government | active | breed | serious | pollution |

1 to mate and produce offspring: _____

2 the act of making water or soil dirty: _____

3 performing a particular physical activity: _____

4 the system of laws and people that control a country: _____

B Find the word that has a similar meaning to the underlined word.

1 You should pay <u>extra</u> money for using the minibar in your room.

    a. bright   *b.* artificial   *c.* additional   *d.* regular

2 According to the police report, the two accidents are closely <u>linked</u>.

    a. related   *b.* divided   *c.* separated   *d.* independent

C Choose the best word to complete each sentence.

1 Don't _____ me with the wrong information.

    a. grow   *b.* depend   *c.* recycle   *d.* confuse

2 It is not easy to keep your _____ on an icy road.

    a. chemical   *b.* balance   *c.* example   *d.* refuge

3 This new construction method was _____ from Japan last year.

    a. reduced   *b.* increased   *c.* respected   *d.* introduced

4 I tightened the cap of the bottle to _____ the juice from leaking.

    a. help   *b.* cause   *c.* prevent   *d.* damage

Odin

We know much about the legends of Greece and Rome but not about those of Northern Europe. However, some famous imaginary characters, such as Santa Claus and Gandalf, are based on one of the gods from those legends: Odin. His name may sound unfamiliar, but Wednesday actually comes from

5 a different spelling of this name — Woden. So who is Odin?

Odin is the greatest god in Northern European legends, whose importance can be compared to that of Zeus, the chief Greek god. According to these legends, his abilities are limitless and his power cannot

be imagined. He rules over war, magic, and even death. He can tell the future and change himself into animals or other shapes. In addition, he has two *ravens that help him rule over the world by flying around and telling him about what is happening. He is also a great warrior and rides an eight-legged horse into battle.

Odin also has a great passion for wisdom. (①) Many legends speak of Odin's endless search for wisdom. (②) In one story, he gave up an eye for a drink of wisdom from a magic well. (③) He died for nine days in order to become wiser by hanging himself from a magic tree. (④) Through these efforts, he gained a great deal of knowledge. That's why Odin is also called _____(A)_____!

*raven: a large black bird of the crow family

1 What is the best title for the passage?

  a. The Origin of Wednesday

  b. Odin: The Wisest Fortune-Teller Ever

  c. The Popularity of Greek and Roman Legends

  d. The Greatest God of Northern European Legends

2 Why does the writer mention <u>Zeus</u>?

  a. To give an example of a wise god

  b. To say that Odin and Zeus are enemies

  c. To explain why Odin is not a popular god

  d. To describe Odin's position among the gods

3 How do the two ravens help Odin rule the world?

_____

4 Where would the following sentence best fit?

After losing his eye, Odin tried an even more reckless quest.

  a. ①   *b.* ②   *c.* ③   *d.* ④

5 What is the best choice for blank (A)?

  a. the lazy learner

  b. the god of wisdom

  c. the master magician

  d. the passionate believer

6 What is NOT mentioned about Odin?

  a. What he rules over

  b. How he became the chief god

  c. What he rides when he goes to war

  d. How he tried to gain more wisdom

Fill in the blanks with the correct words.

Although you may not have heard of him, Odin is an important legendary figure. He has many interesting features, and some famous _____ characters, including Santa Claus and Gandalf, are based on him. He even gets his own day of the week — Wednesday! He is the _____ god of Northern European legends. He has great power and many _____, such as telling the future and changing into different shapes. In addition, his great passion for _____ has led him to do things that hurt his body.

> chief   abilities   wisdom   limitless   imaginary

★ EXPANDING KNOWLEDGE ★

English Dictionary	wise				▼	**Search**

Related Search	awareness judgment	respect wisdom	insight knowledge	philosophy reasonable	depth

Synonyms
- intelligent
- knowledgeable

Antonyms
- ignorant
- foolish
- stupid

Collocations
- a wise act
- a wise decision
- a wise answer
- a wise investment
- wise counsel
- look wise

Write the correct highlighted word next to its definition.

1 fair, practical, and sensible: _____

2 advice and help, especially when given formally: _____

3 the study of theories about knowledge, reality, and existence: _____

4 an opinion or conclusion that you form after thinking carefully: _____

VOCABULARY REVIEW

A Write the correct word next to its definition.

| reckless | well | legend | warrior | quest |

1 a long search or attempt to find something: _____

2 an old story about brave people or adventures: _____

3 a soldier or fighter who is brave or experienced: _____

4 a deep hole in the ground from which people get water: _____

B Find the word that has a similar meaning to the underlined word.

1 Queen Elizabeth I ruled England for 45 years.

    a. praised   *b.* interested   *c.* controlled   *d.* traveled to

2 He was involved in many battles during the war.

    a. games   *b.* countries   *c.* groups   *d.* fights

C Choose the best word to complete each sentence.

1 You can't meet Peter Pan. He is just an _____ character.

    a. evil   *b.* honest   *c.* actual   *d.* imaginary

2 If you come across any _____ words, look them up in the dictionary.

    a. unfamiliar   *b.* basic   *c.* easy   *d.* common

3 As natural resources aren't _____, we have to save them.

    a. powerful   *b.* limitless   *c.* expensive   *d.* restricted

4 The government is making _____ to revive the economy.

    a. errors   *b.* feelings   *c.* efforts   *d.* noises

MATHEMATICS

Before Reading
Do you think of math as useful in everyday life?

Leonardo Fibonacci

1, 2, 3, 4…. As you may know, these numbers are called Arabic numerals. ① This type of numbering system was brought to Europe in the Middle Ages by an Italian mathematician named Fibonacci. ② Up until

5 then, people had used Roman numerals, which were not very practical. ③ Nevertheless, Roman numerals are still used today and can be found in many places. ④ Fibonacci showed that all numbers can be written with just 10 *digits, which can easily be moved and changed to calculate things. This provided the

10 basis for modern mathematics.

    He also developed this sequence: 1, 1, 2, 3, 5, 8, 13, 21, 34, 55, 89, 144…. It's called the Fibonacci sequence, and each number is found by adding the two numbers before it. Actually, it was not Fibonacci who discovered this sequence. It was named

15 after him because he brought it to the West from India. The Fibonacci sequence _____(A)_____. For example, the numbers of petals on flowers and leaves on plants follow the Fibonacci sequence. That's why we can easily find flowers with one, two, three, and five petals. However, flowers with four petals

20 and plants with four leaves — such as lucky four-leaf clovers — are very uncommon.

    As you can see, Fibonacci made many great contributions to mathematics. He is still considered one of the world's greatest mathematicians. Without him,

25 mathematics wouldn't be the same today!

*digit: a written symbol that represents the numbers 0 to 9

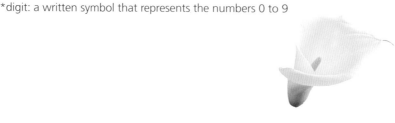

1 What is the passage mainly about?

    a. The mysterious laws of nature

    b. How the Fibonacci sequence was made

    c. A great mathematician and his achievements

    d. The difference between Arabic and Roman numerals

2 Which sentence is NOT needed in the passage?

    a. ①   *b.* ②   *c.* ③   *d.* ④

3 Why was the Fibonacci sequence named after Fibonacci?

_____

4 What is the best choice for blank (A)?

    a. describes many things in nature

    b. is widely used in today's mathematics

    c. teaches us various mathematical formulas

    d. couldn't catch people's attention in the past

5 What can be inferred from the underlined sentence?

    a. Fibonacci guessed correctly how mathematics would change.

    b. Fibonacci had a great effect on the development of mathematics.

    c. Because of Fibonacci, mathematics became as difficult as it is today.

    d. Without Fibonacci, mathematics would've been much more developed.

6 Write T if the statement is true or F if it's false.

    1) Fibonacci introduced Arabic numerals to the West.

    2) Fibonacci was the first to discover a special sequence of numbers.

Fill in the blanks with the correct words.

In the Middle Ages, numerals from the _____ numbering system were brought to Europe by a mathematician named Fibonacci. Fibonacci showed how just 10 digits could be used to make simple calculations. This became the basis for modern mathematics. Furthermore, Fibonacci introduced a number _____ from India wherein each number is the _____ of the two numbers before it, for example, 1, 1, 2, 3, 5, 8, etc. Much of the math found in _____, such as the number of leaves on a plant, follows this sequence.

sum	nature	Arabic	Roman	sequence

★ EXPANDING KNOWLEDGE ★

English Dictionary   calculate   ▼   **Search**

Related Search	numeral	figure	evaluate	angle	accuracy
	add	subtract	multiply	divide	estimate

Synonyms
- count
- compute

Collocations
- calculate an average
- calculate a price
- calculate a total
- calculate in one's head
- accurately calculate
- wrongly calculate

Write the correct highlighted word next to its definition.

1 the quality of being exact and correct: _____

2 to take a number from another number: _____

3 an amount obtained by adding several numbers together: _____

4 the space between two straight lines, which is measured in degrees: _____

VOCABULARY REVIEW

A Write the correct word next to its definition.

basis	petal	modern	numeral	sequence

1 a set of things that have a particular order: _____

2 a written symbol that represents a number: _____

3 a soft colored part around the center of a flower: _____

4 an idea that serves as a foundation for other ideas: _____

B Find the word that has a similar meaning to the underlined word.

1 It is very <u>uncommon</u> for him to come home early.

   a. rare   *b.* polite   *c.* ordinary   *d.* pleasurable

2 None of the students could <u>provide</u> the correct answer.

   a. hide   *b.* give   *c.* describe   *d.* develop

C Choose the best word to complete each sentence.

1 This desert island was _____ by Spanish sailors in 1960.

   a. divided   *b.* counted   *c.* increased   *d.* discovered

2 Skirts aren't _____ when playing sports.

   a. specific   *b.* artificial   *c.* practical   *d.* automatic

3 I quickly _____ the cost, which came out to 50 dollars.

   a. escaped   *b.* employed   *c.* cultivated   *d.* calculated

4 His invention made a big _____ to our modern way of life.

   a. community   *b.* reputation   *c.* organization   *d.* contribution

MEMO

Reading *FORWARD*

INTERMEDIATE 2

★ **Word Book** ★

Unit ★ 01 HISTORY

ash	명 재; 잿더미
predict	동 예측하다, 예견하다
planning	명 계획
blow	동 (바람이) 불다; 불어서 날리다
destroy	동 파괴하다
raise	동 들어올리다; (자금을) 모으다
rebuild	동 재건하다
construct	동 건설하다
construction	명 건설
plenty of	많은, 충분한
architect	명 건축가
architecture	명 건축학
engineer	명 기술자
hire	동 고용하다
modern	형 현대의; 현대적인
steel frame	철골
technique	명 기법, 기술
innovative	형 획기적인
method	명 방법
skyscraper	명 고층 건물
unique	형 독특한
skyline	명 (건물 등이) 하늘과 맞닿은 윤곽선, 스카이라인

barn	명 헛간
spread	동 펼치다; 번지다
out of control	통제할 수 없이
ordinary	형 보통의, 평범한
industrial	형 산업의, 공업의
sightseeing	명 관광
concern	명 중요한 것, 관심사
urban	형 도시의
aspect	명 측면
aesthetic	명 미적 특질
security	명 보안
transportation	명 교통수단
sanitation	명 위생 시설
structure	명 구조
residential	형 주거의
non-residential	형 비주거의
utility	명 공익사업
sewage	명 하수, 오물
treatment	명 치료; 처리
passenger	명 승객
a matter of concern	관심사
disposal	명 처리
facility	명 (pl.) 시설

Unit ★ 02 ORIGINS

skull	몡 두개골, 해골
crossbones	몡 《pl.》 두 개의 뼈를 교차시킨 그림
poisonous	혱 유독한, 독성이 있는
sailor	몡 선원
pirate	몡 해적
piracy	몡 해적 행위
discover	통 발견하다
discovery	몡 발견
in search of	…을 찾아서
wealth	몡 부
establish	통 설립하다
colony	몡 식민지
settle down	정착하다
cattle	몡 소
chase	통 뒤쫓다; 쫓아내다
join	통 연결하다; 합류하다
meanwhile	뷔 그 사이에; 한편
effective	혱 효과적인
rival	몡 경쟁자
control	통 통제하다
navy	몡 해군
protect	통 보호하다

cartoon	몡 만화
logo	몡 로고, 상징
attack	동 공격하다
illegal	혱 불법적인
imagination	몡 상상
fiction	몡 소설, 창작
consist of	…으로 이루어지다
composition	몡 구성
origin	몡 기원
native	혱 원주민의
official	혱 공식적인
background	몡 배경
colonization	몡 식민지화
climate	몡 기후
average	혱 평균의
approve	동 찬성하다, 승인하다
authority	몡 권위; 권위자
typical	혱 전형적인

Unit ★ 03 ART

worth	혱 …의 가치가 있는
value	몡 가치

piece	몡 조각; 작품
focus	동 집중하다
popular culture	대중문화
spread	동 퍼지다, 확산되다
celebrity	몡 유명인사, 연예인
comic book	만화책
inspire	동 영감을 주다
totally	부 완전히, 전적으로
traditionally	부 전통적으로
elite	혱 엘리트의, 엘리트에게 적합한 몡 엘리트 (계층)
have nothing to do with	…와 관계가 없다
challenge	동 도전하다
artistic	혱 예술적인
appeal	동 흥미를 끌다
clearly	부 분명히
thanks to	… 덕분에
classical	혱 고전적인
view	몡 견해; 관점
one-man show	(그림 등의) 개인전
exhibition	몡 전시회
fame	몡 명성
strengthen	동 강화하다
personal	혱 개인의, 개인적인
unusual	혱 특이한

Unit ★ 04 LITERATURE

bishop	몡 주교
receive	통 받다
visit	몡 방문, 문안
stranger	몡 낯선 사람
study	몡 공부; 서재, 연구실
servant	몡 하인
silverware	몡 은 식기류
sigh	통 한숨을 쉬다
belong to	…에 속하다, …의 것이다
obviously	凰 분명히
knock	몡 문 두드리는 소리
greet	통 인사하다, 맞이하다
in a hurry	서둘러
candlestick	몡 촛대
stare	통 쳐다보다
assume	통 추정하다
thief	몡 도둑
theft	몡 도둑질
let ... go	…을 풀어주다
approach	통 …에 다가가다
tremble	통 떨다, 떨리다
grateful	혱 고마워하는

arrest	몡 체포
hide	동 감추다
miserable	혱 불행한, 비참한
novelist	몡 소설가
poet	몡 시인
release	몡 석방
wealthy	혱 부유한
innocent	혱 결백한
remind	동 상기시키다
goodness	몡 선량함
injustice	몡 부당함, 불평등
deed	몡 행위, 행동

Unit ★ 05 FESTIVALS

burnt	혱 불에 탄
gunpowder	몡 화약
celebrate	동 축하하다; 기리다
saint	몡 성인, 성자
carpenter	몡 목수
parade	몡 행진, 퍼레이드
performance	몡 공연
fireworks display	불꽃놀이

firecracker	몡 폭죽
highlight	몡 하이라이트, 가장 흥미로운 부분
resemble	동 닮다
mermaid	몡 인어
huge	형 거대한
candle holder	촛대
practice	몡 관습
set on fire	…에 불을 지르다
flame	몡 불꽃
artwork	몡 예술품
turn	동 돌다; 변하다
impressive	형 인상적인
memory	몡 기억, 추억
emphasize	동 강조하다
setting	몡 배경
spark	몡 불꽃 동 불꽃을 일으키다
flash	몡 섬광, 번쩍임 동 번쩍이다
torch	몡 횃불
glow	몡 (은은한) 불빛 동 (은은히) 빛나다[타다]
burn	몡 화상, 덴 상처 동 (불이) 타오르다
explosion	몡 폭발
crime	몡 범죄
victim	몡 희생자
fuel	몡 연료
blaze	몡 불꽃, 화염

flare	명 확 타오르는 불길[불꽃]
enthusiasm	명 열정
fire alarm	화재 경보기
fire extinguisher	소화기
disastrous	형 처참한
put out	(불 등을) 끄다
illegal	형 불법적인
intense	형 극심한, 강렬한
excitement	명 흥분

Unit ★ 06 FOOD

flag	명 기, 깃발
maple	명 단풍나무
symbol	명 상징(물)
oatmeal	명 오트밀
beer	명 맥주
boil	동 끓이다; 끓다
contain	동 …이 들어[함유되어] 있다
artificial	형 인공의
flavoring	명 향료
classify	동 분류하다
grade	명 등급

recommend	통 추천하다; 권하다
excellence	명 뛰어남
complicated	형 복잡한
spicy	형 양념 맛이 강한
flavor	명 맛
tasty	형 맛있는
yummy	형 아주 맛있는
appetizing	형 식욕을 돋우는
nutritious	형 영양가가 높은
incredibly	부 믿을 수 없을 정도로
substance	명 물질
breathe in	숨을 들이쉬다

Unit ★ 07 PLACES

bury	통 묻다, 매장하다
graveyard	명 묘지
resting place	안식처, 무덤
retire	통 은퇴[퇴직]시키다
major	형 주요한
airline	명 항공사
cargo	명 화물
aircraft	명 항공기

passenger	몡 승객
replace	통 대신하다; 교체하다
damage	통 피해를 입히다
ground	몡 지면, 땅
support	통 받치다, 지탱하다
weight	몡 무게
exotic	톙 외국의; 이국적인
scenery	몡 경치, 풍경
appear	통 나타나다; 출연하다, 등장하다
spot	몡 점; 장소
storage	몡 저장, 보관
pilot	몡 비행사
captain	몡 (항공기의) 기장
flight attendant	승무원
cabin	몡 객실
passport	몡 여권
departure	몡 출발
arrival	몡 도착
craft	몡 항공기
airliner	몡 여객기
crash	몡 추락 통 추락하다
board	통 탑승하다
get off	내리다
take off	이륙하다
land	통 착륙하다

vehicle	몡 차량, 탈것

Unit ★ 08 SPORTS

knock down	쓰러뜨리다
reappear	동 다시 나타나다
religious	형 종교적인
ceremony	몡 의식
priest	몡 사제, 신부
lane	몡 길; (운동 경기의) 레인
devil	몡 악마
weapon	몡 무기
keep away	…을 멀리하다
sin	몡 죄
forgive	동 용서하다
reformer	몡 개혁가
gain	동 얻다
popularity	몡 인기
neglect	동 방치하다, 소홀히 하다
duty	몡 의무; 직무, 임무
ban	동 금지하다
gamble	동 돈을 걸다, 도박을 하다
self-control	몡 자제력

entertainment	몡 오락
military	혱 군대의, 군사의
prohibit	동 금지하다
get around	(법률 따위를) 빠져 나가다
establish	동 제정하다
represent	동 나타내다, 상징하다
well-known	혱 유명한
attraction	몡 매력
trendy	혱 최신 유행의
reputation	몡 평판, 명성
renown	몡 명성
enormous	혱 막대한, 거대한
maintain	동 유지하다
decline	몡 감소, 축소
desirable	혱 바람직한, 호감 가는

Unit ★ 09 JOBS

scent	몡 향기, 향내
perfume	몡 향수
perfumer	몡 조향사, 향수 제조자
spread	동 퍼지다
fall in love with	…에게 반하다

13

magical	혱 마력이 있는
mix	동 섞다
woody	혱 나무의
recognize	동 인지하다, 알아보다
delicate	혱 연약한; 섬세한
creation	몡 창조; 창작품
concept	몡 개념
passion	몡 열정
recipe	몡 요리법, 제조법
quantity	몡 양, 분량
ingredient	몡 재료, 성분
fragrance	몡 향기; 향수
attractive	혱 매력적인
require	동 필요로 하다
course	몡 강의
absolutely	뷔 절대적으로, 무조건
aroma	몡 향기
nerve	몡 신경
sight	몡 시력; 보기, 봄
perceive	동 인지하다
detect	동 감지하다
odor	몡 냄새; 악취
stink	몡 악취 동 악취를 풍기다
stench	몡 악취
disgusting	혱 역겨운, 구역질 나는

faint	휑 희미한
extremely	튄 극도로
become aware of	…을 알게 되다

Unit ★ *10* MEDICINE

poison	명 독
poisonous	휑 독성이 있는
spoil	통 망치다; (음식이) 상하다
nickname	명 별명
fatal	휑 치명적인
toxin	명 독소
gradually	튄 서서히
paralyze	통 마비시키다
muscle	명 근육
dose	명 복용량, 투여량
contract	통 줄어들다, 수축하다
treat	통 다루다, 치료하다
treatment	명 치료
eye doctor	안과 의사
cosmetic	휑 미용의, 화장의
threaten	통 협박하다, 위협하다
disaster	명 참사, 재난

unexpected	혱 예기치 못한
benefit	명 혜택, 이득
affect	동 영향을 미치다
cure	동 치료하다
reduce	동 줄이다
facial	혱 얼굴의
wrinkle	명 주름
venom	명 (뱀 · 거미 등의) 독
protein	명 단백질
heart attack	심장마비
scorpion	명 전갈
promising	혱 유망한, 장래성 있는
government	명 정부
breed	동 새끼를 낳다; 사육하다
be scared of	…을 두려워하다
hairy	혱 털이 많은
insect	명 벌레

Unit ★ 11 ISSUES

charge	동 (요금 · 값을) 청구하다
obese	혱 비만인
obesity	명 비만

fit	⑧ (어떤 장소에 들어가기에) 맞다; 맞추다
debate	⑧ 논의하다
issue	⑲ 문제
right	⑲ 권리
share	⑧ 함께 쓰다; 나누다
discomfort	⑲ 불편 사항
complaint	⑲ 불평, 항의
fix	⑧ 고정시키다; (문제를) 바로잡다
care about	…에 마음을 쓰다
be supposed to-v	…하기로 되어 있다, …해야 한다
ride	⑲ 놀이기구
excess baggage	초과 수하물
vary	⑧ 다르다, 달라지다
burden	⑲ 부담, 짐
rude	⑱ 무례한
offensive	⑱ 모욕적인
overweight	⑱ 과체중인
lack	⑲ 부족
when it comes to	…에 관한 한
embarrassing	⑱ 당황스러운
profit	⑲ 수익
facility	⑲ (pl.) 시설
reasonable	⑱ 타당한
principle	⑲ 원리
flesh	⑲ 살

excessive	형 지나친, 과도한
nutrition	명 영양
greasy	형 기름진
oily	형 기름기가 함유된
store	동 저장하다
layer	명 막, 층
plump	형 통통한
skinny	형 삐쩍 마른
underweight	형 표준 체중 이하의
slim	형 날씬한
lean	형 군살이 없는, 호리호리한
slender	형 날씬한
measurement	명 측정, 측량

Unit ⋆ 12 ANIMALS

play a role	역할을 하다
tiny	형 아주 작은
lonely	형 외로운
paw	명 (동물의 발톱이 달린) 발
shout	동 소리치다
cigarette	명 담배
wrestle	동 레슬링을 하다

mascot	명 마스코트
carry	동 나르다
bomb	명 폭탄
bullet	명 총알
enemy	명 적
spy	명 스파이, 첩자
enlist	동 입대시키다
warrior	명 전사
retire	동 은퇴하다
sculpture	명 조각품
sign	명 징후; 표지판
in memory of	…을 기념하여
intelligence	명 지능
aftermath	명 여파, 후유증
nationalism	명 민족주의, 애국심
invasion	명 침략, 침입
civil war	내전
break out	발발하다
axis	명 축; (제2차 세계 대전 때의) 독일 · 이탈리아 · 일본 추축국
attack	동 공격하다
advance	명 진군
ally	명 동맹국; (세계 대전 때의) 연합국
momentum	명 탄력, 가속도
collapse	동 붕괴되다, 무너지다
impact	명 영향

casualty	명 사상자
concentration camp	강제 수용소
slave labor	강제 노동자
genocide	명 집단 학살
murder	명 살인, 살해
by force	강제로
make peace with	…와 화해하다

Unit★13 ENTERTAINMENT

spotlight	명 환한 조명
merry	형 즐거운
acrobat	명 곡예사
reality	명 현실
magical	형 마법의; 황홀한
world-famous	형 세계적으로 유명한
entertainment	명 오락; 연예
performer	명 연기자
performance	명 공연
perform	동 공연하다
feature	명 특징 동 특징으로 삼다
clown	명 광대
silly	형 바보 같은; 우스꽝스러운

20

hoop	몡 고리; (서커스의 곡예용) 둥근 테
combine	동 결합하다
artistic	혱 예술적인
element	몡 요소
gymnastics	몡 체조
unbelievable	혱 믿기 힘든
trick	몡 속임수; 재주, 묘기
put on	…을 입다[쓰다]; (연극 · 쇼 등을) 무대에 올리다
search for	…을 찾다
athlete	몡 운동선수
attention	몡 주의, 관심
currently	뷔 현재, 지금
aquatic	혱 물속에 사는; 물과 관련된
fantasy	몡 공상, 상상
synchronized swimmer	수중 발레를 하는 사람
instrument	몡 기구; 악기

Unit ★ 14 PSYCHOLOGY

throw away	…을 버리다
trash can	쓰레기통
messy	혱 지저분한
theory	몡 이론

unrepaired	혱 수리되지 않은
repair	동 수리하다
rest	명 나머지
uncared for	돌보지 않은, 방치된
attract	동 끌다, 유인하다
park	동 주차하다
damage	동 손상을 주다 명 손상
disorder	명 무질서
encourage	동 격려하다; 부추기다, 조장하다
neglect	동 방치하다
minor	혱 작은
crime	명 범죄
lead to	…로 이어지다
additional	혱 추가의
pay attention to	…에 유의하다
litter	동 (쓰레기를) 버리다
graffiti	명 낙서
ignore	동 무시하다
uncontrollable	혱 걷잡을 수 없는
violence	명 폭력
proper	혱 적절한
replace	동 대신하다
arrest	동 체포하다
criminal	혱 범죄의 명 범인, 범죄자
suspect	명 용의자 동 의심하다

22

victim	몡 피해자
illegal	몡 불법적인
detective	몡 형사
evidence	몡 증거
judgment	몡 판단; 판결
guilty	몡 유죄의
violation	몡 위반
offence	몡 위법 행위, 범죄
misdeed	몡 악행
violent	몡 폭력적인
commit	몡 저지르다, 범하다
confess	몡 자백하다, 고백하다
witness	몡 목격하다
court	몡 법정

Unit ★ *15* CULTURE

Buddhist	몡 부처의; 불교의
kingdom	몡 왕국
developed	몡 발달한, 선진의
refuge	몡 피난; 위안
religion	몡 종교
standard	몡 기준

measure	통 측정하다, 재다
material	형 물질적인
wealth	명 부, 재산
improve	통 개선하다
healthcare	명 건강관리, 의료 (서비스)
treat	통 대하다; 치료하다
abroad	부 외국으로
protect	통 지키다, 보호하다
regulate	통 규제하다
tourism	명 관광업
licensed	형 허가받은
tour operator	관광업자
agent	명 대리인, 중개인
remain	통 계속 …이다
forested	형 숲으로 뒤덮인
heritage	명 유산
emotional	형 감정적인
state	명 상태
well-being	명 행복, 웰빙
factor	명 요소
influence	통 영향을 미치다
interaction	명 상호작용
accomplishment	명 업적, 공적
subjective	형 주관적인
affect	명 정서 통 영향을 미치다
satisfaction	명 만족

worship	몡 예배, 숭배
regardless of	…에 상관 없이

Unit ★ 16 MYSTERIES

enormous	혱 거대한
mansion	몡 대저택
haunted	혱 유령이 나오는
rifle	몡 소총
manufacturing	혱 제조의
suffer	동 시달리다, 고통받다
spirit	몡 정신; 영혼
shoot	동 (총 등을) 쏘다
gun	몡 총
work on	…에 공을 들이다
staircase	몡 계단, 층계
ceiling	몡 천장
dozens of	수십의, 많은
secret	혱 비밀의
passageway	몡 통로
confuse	동 혼동시키다
evil	혱 나쁜, 사악한
complicated	혱 복잡한

severe	형 엄한; 심한
arthritis	명 관절염
plan	명 계획; 도면, 설계도
inspection	명 검사, 점검
construction	명 건축
tragic	형 비극적인
effective	형 효과적인
escape	동 달아나다, 탈출하다
architect	명 건축가
relieve	동 (고통을) 덜어 주다
supervision	명 감독
horrifying	형 소름 끼치는
illusion	명 환상, 환각
devil	명 악마
soul	명 영혼
ghost	명 귀신
superstition	명 미신
supernatural	형 초자연적인
a restless spirit	죽은 뒤 잠들지 못하는 영혼
force	명 힘, 영향력
spiritual	형 정신의, 정신적인
separate	형 분리된

Unit★*17* TECHNOLOGY

scene	몡 장면
sense	통 느끼다; (기계가) 감지하다
brainwave	몡 뇌파
screen	몡 화면, 스크린
fantasy	몡 환상, 공상
unrealistic	혱 비현실적인
technology	몡 기술
connect	통 연결하다
attach	통 부착하다
interpret	통 해석하다
signal	몡 신호
device	몡 (기계) 장치
control	통 통제하다, 조종하다
operate	통 작동[가동]시키다
draw attention	주의를 끌다
convenient	혱 편리한
convenience	몡 편리
eventually	봄 결국
paralyzed	혱 마비된
advanced	혱 진보된
automatic	혱 자동의
detect	통 발견하다, 감지하다

27

cure	⑧ 치유하다
division	⑲ 분할; 구획
divide	⑧ 나누다
skull	⑲ 두개골
protection	⑲ 보호
function	⑲ 기능
process	⑧ 처리하다
perception	⑲ 지각
metabolism	⑲ 신진대사
stroke	⑲ 타격; 뇌졸중
tumor	⑲ 종양
syndrome	⑲ 증후군
deal with	(문제·과제 등을) 처리하다
have nothing to do with	…와 관계가 없다

Unit ★18 ENVIRONMENT

countryside	⑲ 시골 지역
pollution	⑲ 오염, 공해
link	⑧ 관련 짓다
breast cancer	유방암
chemical	⑲ 화학물질
normally	⑨ 정상적으로

blood pressure	혈압
balance	명 균형
hinder	동 방해하다
threaten	동 협박[위협]하다
confuse	동 혼란시키다
active	형 활동적인
breed	동 새끼를 낳다, 번식하다
encourage	동 격려하다; 권장하다
escape	동 탈출하다; 새어 나가다
sideways	부 옆으로
upwards	부 위쪽으로
fossil fuel	화석 연료
emission	명 배출물, 배출가스
wastewater	명 폐수, 오수
natural disaster	자연재해
excessive	형 과도한
soil	명 흙, 땅
pesticide	명 살충제
reduce	동 줄이다, 축소하다
reuse	동 재사용하다
recycle	동 재활용하다
protocol	명 협정
release	동 방출하다
arrangement	명 합의, 협의
coal	명 석탄

| pollute | 통 오염시키다 |

Unit ★ 19 MYTHOLOGY

legend	명 전설
imaginary	형 가상의
unfamiliar	형 익숙지 않은, 낯선
spelling	명 맞춤법; 철자
chief	형 주된; 최고의
limitless	형 무한한
rule	통 통치하다, 지배하다
warrior	명 전사
battle	명 전투
passion	명 열정
passionate	형 열정적인
endless	형 무한한, 한없는
wisdom	명 지혜
well	명 우물
hang	통 목을 매달다
fortune-teller	명 점쟁이
reckless	형 무모한
quest	명 탐구, 탐색
awareness	명 의식

insight	몡 통찰력, 이해
philosophy	몡 철학
depth	몡 깊이
judgment	몡 판단
reasonable	혱 타당한, 사리에 맞는
knowledgeable	혱 아는 것이 많은
ignorant	혱 무지한
investment	몡 투자
counsel	몡 조언
fair	혱 공정한, 공평한
practical	혱 실질적인; 실용적인; 타당한
sensible	혱 분별 있는, 합리적인
formally	븟 공식적으로
existence	몡 존재
conclusion	몡 결론

Unit ★ 20 MATHEMATICS

numeral	몡 숫자
mathematician	몡 수학자
calculate	똥 계산하다
provide	똥 제공하다
basis	몡 근거; 기반

sequence	몡 순서; 수열
add	동 더하다
discover	동 발견하다
petal	몡 꽃잎
uncommon	형 드문
contribution	몡 기여, 이바지
formula	몡 공식
figure	몡 숫자
evaluate	동 평가하다
angle	몡 각도
accuracy	몡 정확, 정확도
subtract	동 빼다
multiply	동 곱하다
divide	동 나누다
estimate	동 추정하다
count	동 세다; 계산하다
compute	동 계산하다
average	몡 평균
exact	형 정확한
correct	형 옳은
straight	형 곧은, 똑바른
degree	몡 (각도의 단위인) 도

Reading FORWARD

INTERMEDIATE 2

★ Answer Key ★

Reading
FORWARD

INTERMEDIATE 2

★ Answer Key ★

★Chicago City Planning

1 b   **2** c   **3** d   **4** d   **5** some of the world's first skyscrapers were built in Chicago   **6** d

---

화재는 물건들을 태워 재로 만든다. 이는 화재로 모든 것을 잃을 수 있다는 것을 의미한다. 하지만 화재는 또한 새로운 것을 시작할 기회를 만들 수도 있다. 이것은 오래전 시카고에서 일어났던 일이다.

1871년 10월의 어느 날 밤, 시카고 대화재가 시작되었다. 그것은 갑자기 발생했지만, 예견되었던 것일 수도 있다. 화재가 나기 전 40년 동안, 시카고는 거의 계획 없이 빠르게 성장했다. 많은 건물들과 거리들이 나무로 만들어졌다. 더군다나, 1871년의 여름은 매우 건조했다. 그래서, 한 헛간에서 화재가 시작되었을 때, 그것은 통제할 수 없이 빠르게 번졌다. 강한 바람에 날려, 불길은 도시의 중심부를 관통해 지나갔다. 화재가 시작되고 이틀 후, 약 만 8천여 채의 건물들이 파괴되었고 3백 명의 사람들이 사망했다.

화재는 시카고의 3분의 1을 파괴했지만, 이것이 그 도시의 종말은 아니었다. 화재 직후, 도시를 재건하기 위해 5천만 달러가 모금되었다. 이번에는, 건물들이 충분한 계획을 가지고 건설되었다. 최고의 건축가들과 기술자들이 새롭고, 현대적인 도시를 건설하기 위해 고용되었다. 게다가, 최신 철골 기술과 획기적인 건축 방식들이 사용되었다. 이러한 현대 기술 덕분에, 세계 최초의 고층 건물들 중 일부가 시카고에 세워졌다. 그것들은 시카고에 독특한 스카이라인과 아름다움을 선사한다.

오늘날, 많은 관광객들이 시카고를 방문하러 간다. 하지만, 그들 중 이 아름다운 도시가 그야말로 잿더미에서 일어났다는 것을 아는 사람은 거의 없다.

어휘   ash[æʃ] 몡 재; 잿더미   predict[pridíkt] 용 예측하다, 예견하다   planning[plǽniŋ] 몡 계획   blow[blou] 용 (바람이) 불다; *불어서 날리다   destroy[distrɔ́i] 용 파괴하다   raise[reiz] 용 들어 올리다; *(자금을) 모으다   rebuild[rìːbíld] 용 재건하다   construct[kənstrʌ́kt] 용 건설하다 (construction 몡 건설)   plenty of 많은, 충분한   architect[ɑ́ːrkitèkt] 몡 건축가 (architecture 몡 건축학)   engineer[èndʒiníər] 몡 기술자   hire[haiər] 용 고용하다   modern[mɑ́dərn] 혱 현대의; *현대적인   steel frame 철골   technique[tekníːk] 몡 기법, 기술   innovative[ínəvèitiv] 혱 획기적인   method[méθəd] 몡 방법   skyscraper[skáiskrèipər] 몡 고층 건물   unique[juːníːk] 혱 독특한   skyline[skáilàin] 몡 (건물 등이) 하늘과 맞닿은 윤곽선, 스카이라인   [문제] barn[baːrn] 몡 헛간   spread[spred] 용 펼치다; *번지다   out of control 통제할 수 없이   ordinary[ɔ́ːrdənèri] 보통의, 평범한   industrial[indʌ́striəl] 혱 산업의, 공업의   sightseeing[sáitsìːiŋ] 몡 관광

구문   3행   However, a fire can also create an opportunity **to start** *something new.*
- to start: an opportunity를 수식하는 형용사적 용법의 to부정사
- something new: -thing으로 끝나는 대명사는 형용사가 뒤에서 수식함

10행   It happened suddenly, but it **could have been** predicted.
- could have v-ed: '…했을 수도 있다'의 의미로, 과거의 일에 대한 추측을 나타냄

17행   (Being) **Blown** by a strong wind, it moved through the center of the city.
- Blown: 동시동작을 나타내는 분사구문으로, 앞에 Being이 생략되어 있음(= As it was blown)

18행   Two days after the fire began, about 18,000 buildings **had been destroyed**, and 300 people had died.
- had been destroyed: 과거 기준 시점까지의 동작의 완료를 나타내는 과거완료 수동태

STRATEGIC SUMMARY   broke out, spread, rebuild, construction

2

1 *1)* residential *2)* urban *3)* transportation   **2** *1)* F *2)* T

어휘 concern[kənsə́:rn] 똉 중요한 것, 관심사 urban[ə́:rbən] 혱 도시의 aspect[ǽspekt] 똉 측면
aesthetic[esθétik] 똉 미적 특질 security[sikjúərəti] 똉 보안 transportation[trænspərtéiʃən]
똉 교통수단 sanitation[sænitéiʃən] 똉 위생 시설 structure[strʌ́ktʃər] 똉 구조
residential[rèzədénʃəl] 혱 주거의 (non-residential 혱 비주거의) utility[ju:tíləti] 똉 공익사업
sewage[sú:idʒ] 똉 하수, 오물 treatment[trí:tmənt] 똉 치료; *처리 [문제] passenger[pǽsindʒər]
똉 승객 a matter of concern 관심사 disposal[dispóuzəl] 똉 처리 facility[fəsíləti] 똉 《pl.》
시설

VOCABULARY REVIEW

A 1 skyline **2** ash **3** construct **4** barn
B 1 c **2** b   **C 1** c **2** c **3** b **4** d

unit 02 ORIGINS

pp. 12-15

The Caribbean Pirates

1 a **2** It was the symbol for pirates. **3** b **4** a **5** b **6** c

인간의 해골과 교차된 두 개의 뼈 그림을 본 적이 있는가? 오늘날, 그것은 어떤 것이 독성이 있다는 것을 나타낸다. 하지만 18세기 카리브 해의 선원들에게 그것은 해적의 상징이었다! 그렇다면 이러한 해적들은 어디에서 온 것일까?

1492년 콜럼버스가 카리브 해의 섬들을 발견한 후, 많은 유럽인들이 부를 찾고 식민지를 건설하기 위해 그곳에 갔다. 가장 강력한 세력은 스페인이었지만, 다른 나라에서 온 사람들도 그곳에 정착했다. 그들 중에는 카리브 해의 섬들 중 하나인 Hispaniola 섬에 살았던 몇몇 프랑스 사람들도 있었다. 그들은 그 섬에 있는 돼지와 소를 사냥했고, 지나가는 배에 말린 고기를 팔았다. 하지만 그들은 또한 그 배들을 공격하고 훔치기도 했다! 그래서, 스페인 사람들은 그들을 Hispaniola 섬에서 쫓아냈고, 이것은 그들이 스페인 사람들을 싫어하게 만들었다. 그들은 다른 섬에 가서 영국과 네덜란드 선원들에 합류했다. 곧, 그들은 스페인 사람들을 공격하는 해적이 되었다!

한편, 영국과 같은 나라들은 해적을 이용하는 것이 그들의 경쟁자인 스페인을 공격하는 저렴하고 효과적인 방법이라는 것을 알았다. 그래서 그들은 스페인 배와 식민지를 공격하기 위해 해적들을 고용했다. 하지만 해적이 점점 강해지자, 그들은 통제하기 힘들어졌고, 그들은 심지어 원하지 않는 전쟁을 일으키기까지 했다. 결국, 유럽 국가들은 해적 행위를 불법화했고 그들의 식민지를 보호하기 위해 자국의 해군을 만들었다.

오늘날, 카리브 해에는 해적이 없다. 하지만 당신은 그들을 책, 영화, 그리고 만화에서 볼 수 있다. 당신은 또한 그들을 야구팀인 Pittsburgh Pirates의 로고에서도 볼 수 있다!

어휘 skull[skʌl] 똉 두개골, 해골 crossbones[krɔ́:sbòunz] 똉 《pl.》 두 개의 뼈를 교차시킨 그림
poisonous[pɔ́izənəs] 혱 유독한, 독성이 있는 sailor[séilər] 똉 선원 pirate[páirət] 똉 해적 (piracy
똉 해적 행위) discover[diskʌ́vər] 똉 발견하다 (discovery 똉 발견) in search of …을 찾아서
wealth[welθ] 똉 부 establish[istǽbliʃ] 똉 설립하다 colony[káləni] 똉 식민지 settle down
정착하다 cattle[kǽtl] 똉 소 chase[tʃeis] 똉 뒤쫓다; *쫓아내다 join[dʒɔin] 똉 연결하다; *합류하다
meanwhile[mí:nwàil] 뷔 그 사이에; *한편 effective[iféktiv] 혱 효과적인 rival[ráivəl]
똉 경쟁자 control[kəntróul] 똉 통제하다 navy[néivi] 똉 해군 protect[prətékt] 똉 보호하다
cartoon[ka:rtú:n] 똉 만화 logo[lóugou] 똉 로고, 상징 [문제] attack[ətǽk] 똉 공격하다
illegal[ilí:gəl] 혱 불법적인 imagination[imædʒənéiʃən] 똉 상상 fiction[fíkʃən] 똉 소설, 창작
consist of …으로 이루어지다

9행 Among them **were some French people** [*who* lived on Hispaniola Island, …].
- were some French people: 부사구(Among them)가 문장 앞에 와서 주어와 동사가 도치됨
- who 이하는 some French people을 수식하는 주격 관계대명사절

12행 So, the Spanish chased them from Hispaniola, **which** *made* them *hate* the Spanish.
- which: 앞의 절을 선행사로 하는 계속적 용법의 주격 관계대명사
- 사역동사(make) + 목적어 + 동사원형: …가 ~하게 하다

15행 … found that **using pirates** was a cheap and effective way *to attack* their rival, Spain.
- using pirates: that절의 주어로 쓰인 동명사구
- to attack: a cheap and effective way를 수식하는 형용사적 용법의 to부정사

18행 However, as the pirates got stronger, they became hard **to control**, ….
- to control: 형용사 hard를 수식하는 부사적 용법의 to부정사

STRATEGIC ORGANIZER   hunting, chased, rival, illegal

EXPANDING KNOWLEDGE

1 *1)* official   *2)* climate   *3)* native   **2**   *1)* F   *2)* T

어휘   composition[kàmpəzíʃən] 명 구성   origin[ɔ́:rədʒin] 명 기원   native[néitiv] 형 원주민의
official[əfíʃəl] 형 공식적인   background[bǽkgràund] 명 배경   colonization[kàlənizéiʃən]
명 식민지화   climate[kláimit] 명 기후   average[ǽvəridʒ] 형 평균의   [문제] approve[əprú:v]
동 찬성하다, 승인하다   authority[əθɔ́:rəti] 명 권위; 권위자   typical[típikəl] 형 전형적인

VOCABULARY REVIEW

A **1** hunt **2** logo **3** colony **4** skull
B **1** d **2** c   **C** **1** c **2** b **3** b **4** d

⋆unit⋆ 03 ART

pp. 16-19

⋆Pop Art

1 c **2** c **3** d **4** something that was elite and had nothing to do with ordinary things **5** d
6 *1)* F *2)* T

뉴욕에 있는 현대 미술관을 방문하면, 당신은 32개의 평범한 수프 통조림 그림을 발견할 것이다. 그것은 매우 단순해서, 당신은 아마도 그것을 특별한 것으로 여기지 않을 것이다. 하지만 그것이 천백만 달러가 넘는 가치가 있다는 것을 알면 당신은 아마 놀랄 것이다! (예술품의 진정한 가치는 돈과 전혀 관계가 없다.) 사실, 그것은 지금까지 만들어진 가장 유명한 팝 아트 작품들 중 하나이다.

팝 아트는 popular art의 줄임말이다. 그것은 대중문화에 초점을 둔 예술을 일컫는다. 그것은 1950년대에 영국과 미국에서 시작되어 전 세계로 퍼졌다. 팝 아트는 유명인사, 광고, 만화책, 영화, 그리고 텔레비전 쇼와 같은 일상적인 주제에 집중한다. 앤디 워홀과 로이 릭턴스타인을 포함한 많은 유명한 팝 아트 작가들이 있다. 워홀은 유명한 사람이나 사물들의 이미지를 이용하여, 종종 그것들을 모방하고 색을 변화시키는 것으로 알려져 있다. 한편, 릭턴스타인은 만화에서 영감을 받은 그림들로 유명하다.

팝 아트는 일상생활에 대한 완전히 새롭고 신선한 시각을 제공하기 때문에 흥미롭고 인기가 있다. 전통적으로, 예술은 엘리트에게 적합하고 평범한 것들과는 관계가 없는 것으로 여겨졌다. 그러나 팝 아트는 이러한 생각에 도전한다. 그것은 사람들이 일상생활에서 보는 이미지를 예술적이고 흥미로운 것으로 바꾸어 놓는다. 그것이 팝 아티스트들의 작품이 모든 사람의 흥미를 끄는 이유이다. 분명, 팝 아트 덕분에, 예술은 대중에게 더 친근해졌다!

어휘 worth[wəːrθ] 휑 …의 가치가 있는　value[vǽljuː] 명 가치　piece[piːs] 명 조각; *작품
focus[fóukəs] 동 집중하다　popular culture 대중문화　spread[spred] 동 퍼지다, 확산되다
celebrity[səlébrəti] 명 유명인사, 연예인　comic book 만화책　inspire[inspáiər] 동 영감을 주다
totally[tóutəli] 부 완전히, 전적으로　traditionally[trədíʃənəli] 부 전통적으로　elite[ilíːt]
휑 엘리트의, 엘리트에게 적합한 명 엘리트 (계층)　have nothing to do with …와 관계가
없다　challenge[tʃǽlindʒ] 동 도전하다　artistic[aːrtístik] 휑 예술적인　appeal[əpíːl] 동 흥미를
끌다　clearly[klíərli] 부 분명히　thanks to … 덕분에　[문제] classical[klǽsikəl] 휑 고전적인
view[vjuː] 명 견해; *관점

구문 5행　However, you may be surprised **to learn** that it is worth more than 11 million dollars!
　　• to learn: '…한다면'의 의미로, 조건을 나타내는 부사적 용법의 to부정사
10행　It refers to art [**that** focuses on popular culture].
　　• that 이하는 art를 수식하는 주격 관계대명사절
16행　Warhol **is known for** [*using* images of famous people and things], often [**copying** them] and [**changing** their colors].
　　• be known for: …로 알려져 있다
　　• using 이하는 전치사 for의 목적어 역할을 하는 동명사구
　　• copying과 changing 이하는 동시동작을 나타내는 분사구문
25행　That's (the reason) **why** the work of pop artists appeals to everyone.
　　• why: 이유를 나타내는 관계부사로, 앞에 선행사 the reason이 생략되어 있음

STRATEGIC SUMMARY　celebrities, challenged, common, popularity

EXPANDING KNOWLEDGE

1 c　**2** 1) F　2) T

　　예술가 앤디 워홀은 1928년에 태어났고 27세의 나이에 그의 첫 개인전을 가졌다. 1956년에, 그는 뉴욕 현대 미술관에서 열린 주요 전시회의 일원이었다. 하지만 그의 진정한 성공은 1960년대에 왔다. 그는 마릴린 먼로와 캠벨 수프의 통조림과 같은 대중문화에서 가져온 사람과 사물의 이미지를 만들어내는 것으로 유명해졌다. 그의 명성은 또한 그의 이상한 개인 생활에 의해서 강화되었다. 그는 돈을 흥청망청 썼고, 부유한 사람들과 어울리기 좋아했으며, 독특한 의상을 입었다. 워홀은 1987년에 사망했지만, 그는 여전히 '팝 아트의 왕자'로 기억된다.

어휘 one-man show (그림 등의) 개인전　exhibition[èksəbíʃən] 명 전시회　fame[feim] 명 명성
strengthen[stréŋkθən] 동 강화하다　personal[pə́rsənl] 휑 개인의, 개인적인　unusual[ʌnjúːʒuəl]
휑 특이한

구문 4행　He became famous for [**creating** images of people and things from popular culture], ….
　　• creating 이하는 전치사 for의 목적어 역할을 하는 동명사구

VOCABULARY REVIEW

A **1** elite　**2** appeal　**3** inspire　**4** focus
B **1** d　**2** d　　**C** **1** b　**2** d　**3** a　**4** c

unit 04 LITERATURE

pp. 20-23

★Jean Valjean

1 d **2** d **3** d **4** b **5** He wanted Jean Valjean to use the money from the silverware to become an honest man. **6** b

어느 날, 주교는 장 발장이라는 이름의 가난한 낯선 이의 방문을 받았다. 다음 날 아침, 하인이 그를 부르는 것을 들었을 때 그는 자신의 서재에 있었다.

"주교님! 그 낯선 이가 사라졌고 우리 은 식기도 없어졌어요! 그가 그것을 훔쳐간 것이 틀림없어요!"라고 하인은 외쳤다. 주교는 잠시 생각하더니 한숨을 쉬었다. "그 은 식기가 정말 우리 것이었나요?"라고 그는 물었다. "나는 그것이 누구든 그것을 가장 필요로 하는 사람의 것이라고 생각해요. 그리고 분명 가난한 사람이 나보다 그것을 더 필요로 할 겁니다. 그가 그것을 가져간 것이 정말 잘못인가요?"

바로 그때 문을 두드리는 소리가 났다. 주교가 문을 열었을 때, 그는 세 명의 경찰관이 장 발장을 붙잡고 있는 것을 보았다. 주교는 웃으면서 장을 맞이했다. "거기 계셨군요! 너무 서둘러 가셨어요. 제가 드린 은 촛대를 잊으셨군요!" 장은 매우 놀라서 주교를 쳐다보았다. 경찰관들 역시 놀란 것처럼 보였다. "그럼, 그가 사실을 말했던 겁니까?"라고 한 사람이 물었다. "우리는 그가 은 식기가 든 가방을 들고 거리를 달려오는 것을 보고, 그가 도둑이라고 생각했어요." "유감이지만 오해가 있었던 것 같네요."라고 주교는 말했다. "그를 놓아주세요."

경찰관들이 떠난 후에, 장은 주교에게 다가갔다. 그의 온몸은 떨리고 있었다. "정말이세요? 제가 가도 되나요?"라고 그는 물었다. "네."라고 주교는 말했다. "하지만 이 은 식기로 얻는 돈을 정직한 사람이 되기 위해 쓰는 것을 잊지 마세요." 장은 너무 고마워서 아무 말도 떠올릴 수 없었다.

어휘   bishop[bíʃəp] 명 주교   receive[risí:v] 동 받다   visit[vízit] 명 방문, 문안   stranger[stréindʒər] 명 낯선 사람   study[stʌ́di] 명 공부; *서재, 연구실   servant[sə́:rvənt] 명 하인   silverware[sílvərwɛ̀ər] 명 은 식기류   sigh[sai] 동 한숨을 쉬다   belong to …에 속하다, …의 것이다   obviously[ábviəsli] 부 분명히   knock[nak] 명 문 두드리는 소리   greet[gri:t] 동 인사하다, 맞이하다   in a hurry 서둘러   candlestick[kǽndlstìk] 명 촛대   stare[stɛər] 동 쳐다보다   assume[əsú:m] 동 추정하다   thief[θi:f] 명 도둑 (theft 명 도둑질)   let ... go …을 풀어주다   approach[əpróutʃ] 동 …에 다가가다   tremble[trémbl] 동 떨다, 떨리다   grateful[gréitfəl] 형 고마워하는   [문제] arrest[ərést] 명 체포   hide[haid] 동 감추다

구문

6행   The stranger is gone and **so is our silverware**!
  - so + 동사 + 주어: '…도 또한 그렇다'라는 의미로, so가 맨 앞에 나와서 주어와 동사가 도치됨

7행   He **must have stolen** it!
  - must have v-ed: …했음에 틀림없다

11행   I think it belongs to **whoever** needs it most.
  - whoever: '누구든 …하는 사람'이라는 의미의 복합관계대명사(= anyone who)

21행   When we **saw** him **running** down the street with ....
  - 지각동사(see) + 목적어 + v-ing: …가 ~하고 있는 것을 보다

27행   Jean was **so** grateful **that** he was unable to think of anything to say.
  - so ... that ~: 너무 …해서 ~하다

STRATEGIC SUMMARY   stole, belonged to, assumed, honest

EXPANDING KNOWLEDGE

1 a   **2** *1)* T *2)* F

6

영어로 '불행한 사람들'을 의미하는 *레 미제라블*은 위대한 프랑스 소설가이자 시인인 빅토르 위고가 쓴 유명한 19세기 소설이다. 그것은 장 발장이라는 이름의 도둑에 관한 이야기를 전한다. 그는 빵을 훔친 것 때문에 19년 동안 투옥된다. 석방된 후에, 그는 세상에 대한 분노로 가득 차 있다. 그러나 주교에 의해 경찰로부터 구해지고 난 후, 그는 정직한 사람이 되기로 결심한다. 결국, 그는 부유해지고 성공하게 된다. 그는 또한 결백한 사람을 구하고, 가난한 어린 소녀를 딸로 키운다. 소설은 우리에게 선(善)과 사회적 불평등에 대해 다시 생각하게 한다.

어휘   miserable[mízərəbl] 형 불행한, 비참한   novelist[návəlist] 명 소설가   poet[póuit] 명 시인
release[rilíːs] 명 석방   wealthy[wélθi] 형 부유한   innocent[ínəsənt] 형 결백한
remind[rimáind] 동 상기시키다   goodness[gúdnis] 명 선량함   injustice[indʒʌ́stis] 명 부당함,
불평등   [문제] deed[diːd] 명 행위, 행동

구문   2행   ..., is a famous 19th-century novel [**written** by the great French novelist and
poet Victor Hugo].
• written 이하는 a famous 19th-century novel을 수식하는 과거분사구
6행   However, [**after being saved** from police by a bishop], he decides to be an
honest man.
• after being saved 이하는 때를 나타내는 분사구문으로, 의미를 명확하게 하기 위해 접속사를
생략하지 않음

VOCABULARY REVIEW
A   *1* grateful   *2* thief   *3* approach   *4* honest
B   *1* b   *2* a   C   *1* c   *2* b   *3* a   *4* c

★unit★ 05 FESTIVALS
pp. 24-27

★Las Fallas
1 b   **2** They were throwing firecrackers in the street.   **3** a   **4** b   **5** a   **6** *1)* F   *2)* T

회색 연기가 공중을 메웠다! 나는 가는 곳마다 화약 타는 냄새를 맡았다. 나는 스페인의 발렌시아에서 Las Fallas를 즐기고 있었다! 발렌시아어로 '불'을 의미하는 Las Fallas는 스페인의 가장 큰 축제 중 하나이다. 그것은 목수의 성자인 성 Joseph을 기리기 위해 시작되었다.

3월 19일 성 Joseph의 날이 오기 전 닷새 동안, 많은 퍼레이드와 음악 공연, 그리고 거리 파티가 있었다. 또한, 매일 오후 2시에는 불꽃놀이 쇼가 열렸다. 사람들은 거리에서 폭죽을 던지고 있었다. 나는 강력한 소리 때문에 내 몸이 흔들리는 것을 느낄 수 있었다!

축제의 하이라이트는 ninot을 태우는 것이었다. ninot은 종이와 나무로 만들어진 커다란 인형이다. 그것들은 용, 인어, 그리고 천사와 같은 많은 다양한 것들을 닮았다. 그것들은 아주 커서 내가 *걸리버 여행기*라는 책 속에 있는 것처럼 느껴졌다. 놀랍게도, 어떤 것들은 무려 높이가 20미터였다! ninot을 태우는 전통은 중세 시대에서 비롯되었다. 그 당시에, 목수들은 봄을 맞이하기 위해 나무로 된 촛대를 태우곤 했다. 이후에, 이 관습은 성 Joseph의 날에 거행되었다. 오늘날 사람들은 촛대 대신 ninot을 태운다.

ninot에 불이 붙었을 때, 내가 여태껏 본 것 중 가장 큰 불꽃이 하늘로 솟아올랐다! 그런 아름다운 예술품이 재로 변하는 것을 보는 것이 조금 슬펐지만, 그것은 나에게 스페인에서의 가장 인상적인 추억을 남겨 주었다.

어휘   burnt[bəːrnt] 형 불에 탄   gunpowder[gʌ́npaudər] 명 화약   celebrate[séləbrèit] 동 축하하다;
*기리다   saint[seint] 명 성인, 성자   carpenter[káːrpəntər] 명 목수   parade[pəréid]

명 행진, 퍼레이드　performance[pərfɔ́ːrməns] 명 공연　fireworks display 불꽃놀이
firecracker[fáiərkrækər] 명 폭죽　highlight[háilàit] 명 하이라이트, 가장 흥미로운 부분
resemble[rizémbl] 동 닮다　mermaid[mə́ːrmèid] 명 인어　huge[hjuːʤ] 형 거대한　candle
holder 촛대　practice[prǽktis] 명 관습　set on fire …에 불을 지르다　flame[fleim] 명 불꽃
artwork[áːrtwə̀ːrk] 명 예술품　turn[təːrn] 동 돌다; *변하다　impressive[imprésiv] 형 인상적인
memory[méməri] 명 기억, 추억　[문제] emphasize[émfəsàiz] 동 강조하다　setting[sétiŋ] 명 배경

구문　15행　I could **feel** my body **shake** from the powerful sounds!
　　　　　　• 지각동사(feel) + 목적어 + 동사원형: …이 ~하는 것을 느끼다
　　　17행　Ninots are large dolls [**made of** paper and wood].
　　　　　　• made of 이하는 large dolls를 수식하는 과거분사구
　　　19행　They were **so** huge **that** I *felt like* I was in the book *Gulliver's Travels*!
　　　　　　• so … that ~: 너무 …해서 ~하다
　　　　　　• feel like: …인 것처럼 느끼다
　　　20행　**To my surprise**, some were even 20 meters tall!
　　　　　　• to one's surprise: 놀랍게도
　　　27행　**It** was a little sad [**to see** such beautiful artwork turn to ashes], ….
　　　　　　• It은 가주어이고, to see 이하가 진주어

STRATEGIC SUMMARY　celebrate, performances, burning, artwork

EXPANDING KNOWLEDGE

1 crime　**2** fire extinguisher　**3** enthusiasm　**4** fuel

어휘　spark[spaːrk] 명 불꽃 동 불꽃을 일으키다　flash[flæʃ] 명 섬광, 번쩍임 동 번쩍이다　torch[tɔːrtʃ]
　　　명 횃불　glow[glou] 명 (은은한) 불빛 동 (은은히) 빛나다[타다]　burn[bəːrn] 명 화상, 덴 상처
　　　동 (불이) 타오르다　explosion[iksplóuʒən] 명 폭발　crime[kraim] 명 범죄　victim[víktim]
　　　명 희생자　fuel[fjúːəl] 명 연료　blaze[bleiz] 명 불꽃, 화염　flare[flɛər] 명 확 타오르는 불길[불꽃]
　　　enthusiasm[inθúːziæzm] 명 열정　fire alarm 화재 경보기　fire extinguisher 소화기
　　　disastrous[dizǽstrəs] 형 처참한　put out (불 등을) 끄다　[문제] illegal[ilíːgəl] 형 불법적인
　　　intense[inténs] 형 극심한, 강렬한　excitement[iksáitmənt] 명 흥분

VOCABULARY REVIEW

A　**1** carpenter　**2** highlight　**3** celebrate　**4** flame
B　**1** c　**2** b　　　C　**1** a　**2** c　**3** d　**4** b

unit
06 **FOOD**

pp. 28-31

★*Maple Syrup*

1 c　**2** Because there are lots of maple trees all across the country.　**3** d　**4** b　**5** d　**6** 1) T　2) F

> 캐나다 국기를 본 적이 있는가? 그 중앙에는, 커다란 붉은색 단풍잎이 있다. 전국에 걸쳐 많은 단풍나무가 있기
> 때문에 그것이 캐나다의 상징으로 선정되었다. 캐나다 사람들은 맛있는 메이플 시럽을 만드는 것과 같이, 많은 것들에
> 단풍나무를 이용한다!

메이플 시럽은 수백 년 동안 캐나다 문화의 일부분이었다. 그것은 북동부에 사는 원주민들에 의해서 처음 만들어졌다. 오늘날, 세계 메이플 시럽의 약 85퍼센트가 캐나다에서 나온다. 캐나다 사람들은 메이플 시럽을 너무 좋아해서 그것을 와플, 팬케이크, 오트밀, 제과류와 함께 먹고, 심지어 맥주에도 넣는다.

이 인기 있는 시럽은 수액을 끓여서 만드는데, 그것은 단풍나무에서 모아진다. 수액에는 약 3퍼센트의 당분과 많은 수분이 함유되어 있다. 그것은 수분이 끓어 증발되면서 더 진해지고 더 달아진다. 그것에 약 66퍼센트의 당분이 함유되면, 시럽이 된다! 이런 방식으로 생산되지 않거나 인공 메이플 향료를 포함한 시럽은 메이플 시럽이라고 불릴 수 없다.

캐나다에서, 갓 만들어진 시럽은 그것의 색깔에 따라 1등급에서 3등급까지 분류된다. 숫자가 높을수록, 시럽이 더 짙다! 옅은 색 시럽은 주로 사탕 제조용으로 쓰이고, 짙은 색 시럽은 제빵용이나 요리용으로 권장된다. 아직 메이플 시럽을 먹어본 적이 없다면, 꼭 팬케이크에 그것을 얹어 먹어 보아라. 그러면 왜 캐나다 사람들이 그것을 그렇게 많이 좋아하는지 이해하게 될 것이다!

어휘 flag[flæg] 명 기, 깃발　maple[méipl] 명 단풍나무　symbol[símbəl] 명 상징(물)
oatmeal[óutmìːl] 명 오트밀　beer[biər] 명 맥주　boil[bɔil] 동 끓이다; 끓다　contain[kəntéin] 동 …이 들어[함유되어] 있다　artificial[àːrtəfíʃəl] 형 인공의　flavoring[fléivəriŋ] 명 향료
classify[klǽsəfài] 동 분류하다　grade[greid] 명 등급　recommend[rèkəménd] 동 추천하다;
*권하다　[문제] excellence[éksələns] 명 뛰어남　complicated[kámpləkèitid] 형 복잡한

구문 7행 It was first made by native people [**living** in the Northeast].
　• living 이하는 native people을 수식하는 현재분사구
13행 This popular syrup is made by boiling sap, **which** is collected from maple trees.
　• which: sap을 보충 설명하는 계속적 용법의 주격 관계대명사(= and it)
17행 Syrup [**that**'s not produced this way or includes artificial maple flavoring] can't be called maple syrup.
　• that 이하는 Syrup을 수식하는 주격 관계대명사절
20행 **The higher** the number, **the darker** the syrup!
　• the + 비교급 …, the + 비교급 ~: …하면 할수록, 더욱 ~하다
22행 If you **have**n't **eaten** maple syrup yet, be sure to try it on pancakes.
　• have eaten: '…한 적이 있다'의 의미로, 경험을 나타내는 현재완료

STRATEGIC ORGANIZER　native, collected, boiling, Classified

EXPANDING KNOWLEDGE

1 spicy　**2** fresh　**3** nutritious　**4** smell

어휘 spicy[spáisi] 형 양념 맛이 강한　flavor[fléivər] 명 맛　tasty[téisti] 형 맛있는　yummy[jʌ́mi] 형 아주 맛있는　appetizing[ǽpətàiziŋ] 형 식욕을 돋우는　nutritious[njuːtríʃəs] 형 영양가가 높은
incredibly[inkrédəbli] 부 믿을 수 없을 정도로　[문제] substance[sʌ́bstəns] 명 물질　breathe in 숨을 들이쉬다

VOCABULARY REVIEW

A　**1** artificial　**2** symbol　**3** maple　**4** flavoring
B　**1** a　**2** b　　C　**1** a　**2** d　**3** c　**4** d

07 PLACES

pp. 32-35

★The Airplane Graveyard

1 b **2** Because airlines won't need them for some time or maybe ever again. **3** c **4** a, d
5 d **6** 1) T 2) F

사람들은 죽으면, 묘지에 묻힌다. 하지만 비행기가 더 이상 사용되지 않으면 어디로 갈까? 한 장소는 캘리포니아에 있는 모하비 사막의 비행기 묘지이다. 그곳은 업무에서 은퇴한 수백 대의 비행기들의 안식처이다.

그러면 이 비행기들은 어디에서 올까? 주로 주요 항공사에서 온다. 항공사들은 얼마 동안 또는 어쩌면 다시는 그 비행기들이 필요하지 않을 것이기 때문에 그것들은 모하비로 보내진다. 어떤 비행기들은 단지 몇 달간 머무르지만, 반면에 다른 비행기들은 그곳에서 수년을 머무른다. 하지만 그것들 모두가 정말 '죽은' 것은 아니다. 어떤 비행기들은 화물기로 두 번째 삶을 시작할 기회를 얻는다. 그리고 그것들 중 소수는 여객 수송 업무로 되돌아간다. 물론, 그것들은 안전하다는 것을 확실히 하기 위해 신중히 점검을 받아야 한다. 다른 것들은 때때로 여전히 비행을 하고 있는 비행기들의 부품을 교체하는 데 사용될 수도 있다.

그렇게 많은 거대한 비행기들이 사막 한가운데 있는 것을 보는 것은 낯설지만, 모하비는 그것들에게 완벽한 장소이다. 이는 날씨가 매우 건조하고 맑아서, 비행기들이 날씨에 의해 손상을 입지 않기 때문이다. 또한, 모하비의 땅은 자연적으로 매우 단단하다. 그래서 그것은 거대한 비행기들의 무게를 쉽게 지탱할 수 있다.

광활한 사막과 낡은 비행기들은 이 장소에 이국적인 광경을 준다. 이런 경치 덕분에, 모하비의 비행기 묘지는 많은 영화들에 등장했고, 관광객들은 비행기들을 보려고 그곳으로 여행을 간다.

어휘 bury[béri] ⑧ 묻다, 매장하다 graveyard[gréivjɑ̀ːrd] ⑲ 묘지 resting place 안식처, 무덤
retire[ritáiər] ⑧ 은퇴[퇴직]시키다 major[méidʒər] ⑲ 주요한 airline[ɛ́ərlàin] ⑲ 항공사
cargo[kɑ́ːrgou] ⑲ 화물 aircraft[ɛ́ərkræ̀ft] ⑲ 항공기 passenger[pǽsəndʒər] ⑲ 승객
replace[ripléis] ⑧ 대신하다; *교체하다 damage[dǽmidʒ] ⑧ 피해를 입히다 ground[graund]
⑲ 지면, 땅 support[səpɔ́ːrt] ⑧ 받치다, 지탱하다 weight[weit] ⑲ 무게 exotic[igzátik]
⑲ 외국의; *이국적인 scenery[síːnəri] ⑲ 경치, 풍경 appear[əpíər] ⑧ 나타나다; *출연하다, 등장하다
[문제] spot[spat] ⑲ 점; *장소 storage[stɔ́ːridʒ] ⑲ 저장, 보관

구문 6행 It's a resting place for hundreds of planes [**that** have been retired from service].
　　　　• that 이하는 hundreds of planes를 수식하는 주격 관계대명사절
　　14행 **Some planes** only stay a few months, *while* **others** stay there for years.
　　　　• some … others ~: 어떤 것[사람]들은 …, 다른 것[사람]들은 ~
　　　　• while: '반면에'라는 의미의 접속사
　　16행 Some planes get a chance **to start** a second life as cargo aircraft.
　　　　• to start: a chance를 수식하는 형용사적 용법의 to부정사
　　20행 Although **it**'s strange [**to see** so many giant airplanes *sitting* in the middle of the desert], ….
　　　　• it은 가주어이고, to see 이하가 진주어
　　　　• 지각동사(see) + 목적어 + v-ing: …가 ~하고 있는 것을 보다

STRATEGIC SUMMARY retired, carry, replacement, climate

EXPANDING KNOWLEDGE

1 board **2** departure **3** land **4** cabin

어휘 pilot[páilət] ⑲ 비행사 captain[kǽptən] ⑲ (항공기의) 기장 flight attendant 승무원

10

cabin[kǽbin] 명 객실   passport[pǽspɔ:rt] 명 여권   departure[dipá:rtʃər] 명 출발   arrival[əráivəl]
명 도착   craft[kræft] 명 항공기   airliner[Éərlàinər] 명 여객기   crash[kræʃ] 명 추락 동 추락하다
board[bɔ:rd] 동 탑승하다   get off 내리다   take off 이륙하다   land[lænd] 동 착륙하다
[문제] vehicle[ví:ikl] 명 차량, 탈것

VOCABULARY REVIEW

A *1* aircraft *2* appear *3* retire *4* cargo
B *1* b *2* d   **C** *1* b *2* c *3* d *4* b

★unit★ 08 SPORTS

pp. 36-39

★Bowling

1 c **2** They believed that all their sins would be forgiven. **3** c **4** c **5** d **6** *1)* T *2)* F

스트라이크! 당신의 공이 모든 핀을 쓰러뜨리면 신이 난다. 볼링은 현대 스포츠처럼 보이지만, 그것이 수천 년의 역사를 가지고 있다는 것을 알면 당신은 놀랄지도 모른다. 볼링의 최초 형태는 고대 이집트에서 시작되었다고 믿어진다.

서기 300년경에 볼링은 독일에서 재등장했다. 그 당시에, 그것은 사제들에 의해 행해진 종교적 의식이었다. 그들은 긴 레인 위에서 둥근 돌과 몇 개의 나무 핀들을 사용해서 볼링을 했다. 사제들은 핀을 악마로, 돌은 그들을 물리치는 무기로 여겼다. 그들은 모든 핀을 쓰러뜨리면, 자신들의 모든 죄가 용서될 것이라 믿었다.

시간이 지나면서, 볼링은 교회 밖 사람들에게 소개되었다. 하지만 이번에 그것은 오락으로 여겨졌다! 모두가 볼링을 치는 것을 좋아했다. 그것은 아주 인기가 있어서 유럽 전역으로 퍼졌고 그다음에는 다른 나라들로도 퍼졌다. 심지어 유명한 개혁가인 마틴 루터는 그것의 열성 팬이었고, 그는 핀의 수를 9개로 정했다.

그러나 볼링이 인기를 얻어감에 따라, 그것은 문제를 일으키기 시작했다. 예를 들어, 영국에서는 군인들이 볼링 때문에 종종 자신들의 임무를 소홀히 해서, 왕 에드워드 3세는 그것을 금지했다. 나중에, 미국에서 사람들은 재미뿐만 아니라, 도박 게임을 하기 위해 볼링을 치기 시작했다. 그 결과, 볼링은 불법이 되었다. <u>그러나 법은 오직 9핀 볼링만을 금지했기 때문에, 사람들은 이 법을 피하기 위해서 10번째 핀을 추가했다.</u> 그렇게 해서 현대의 10핀 볼링이 시작되었다! 오늘날, 그것은 세계에서 가장 인기 있는 스포츠 중 하나이다.

어휘 knock down 쓰러뜨리다   reappear[rì:əpíər] 동 다시 나타나다   religious[rilídʒəs] 형 종교적인
ceremony[sérəmòuni] 명 의식   priest[pri:st] 명 사제, 신부   lane[lein] 명 길; *(운동 경기의) 레인
devil[dévl] 명 악마   weapon[wépən] 명 무기   keep away …을 멀리하다   sin[sin] 명 죄
forgive[fərgív] 동 용서하다   reformer[rifɔ́:rmər] 명 개혁가   gain[gein] 동 얻다
popularity[pàpjulǽrəti] 명 인기   neglect[niglékt] 동 방치하다, 소홀히 하다   duty[djú:ti]
명 의무; *직무, 임무   ban[bæn] 동 금지하다   gamble[gǽmbl] 동 돈을 걸다, 도박을 하다
[문제] self-control[sèlfkəntróul] 명 자제력   entertainment[èntərtéinmənt] 명 오락
military[mílitèri] 형 군대의, 군사의   prohibit[prouhíbit] 동 금지하다   get around (법률 따위를)
빠져 나가다   establish[istǽbliʃ] 동 제정하다   represent[rèprizént] 동 나타내다, 상징하다

구문 2행   ..., but you may be surprised **to learn** that it has thousands of years of history.
• to learn: '…한다면'의 의미로, 조건을 나타내는 부사적 용법의 to부정사
     3행   **It** is believed [**that** the first form of bowling was started in ancient Egypt].
• It은 가주어이고, that 이하가 진주어
         7행   The priests **thought of** the pins **as** devils and (thought of) *the rock* **as** a weapon
to keep them **away**.
• think of A as B: A를 B로 여기다

- the rock 앞에 반복되는 부분인 thought of가 생략됨
  - to keep ... away: a weapon을 수식하는 형용사적 용법의 to부정사구
19행 That's **how**[the way] modern ten-pin bowling began!
  - how: 방법을 나타내는 관계부사로, 선행사 the way와는 함께 쓰지 않음

STRATEGIC SUMMARY forgiven, banned, popularity, added

EXPANDING KNOWLEDGE

1 celebrity **2** trendy **3** attraction **4** decline

어휘 well-known[wélnóun] 형 유명한 attraction[ətrǽkʃən] 명 매력 trendy[tréndi] 형 최신 유행의 reputation[rèpjutéiʃən] 명 평판, 명성 renown[rináun] 명 명성 enormous[inɔ́:rməs] 형 막대한, 거대한 maintain[meintéin] 동 유지하다 decline[dikláin] 명 감소, 축소 [문제] desirable[dizáiərəbl] 형 바람직한, 호감 가는

VOCABULARY REVIEW

A **1** ban **2** weapon **3** neglect **4** priest
B **1** b **2** c   **C** **1** a **2** c **3** d **4** d

09 JOBS

pp. 40-43

★Follow Your Nose!

1 c **2** a, d **3** they turn a certain feeling or image into a creation **4** c **5** c **6** a

> 코로 향수의 향기를 들이마시고, 그 느낌이 당신의 몸에 퍼지게 하라. 이것이 내가 조향사로서 하는 일이다. 나는 향수의 마력에 푹 빠졌다. 그것이 내가 조향사가 된 이유이다.
>
> 조향사는 다양한 향기를 섞어서 아름다운 향수를 만든다. 우리는 감귤류의 신선한 향과 숲의 나무 향 같은 수천 가지의 향을 알고 있다. 그리고 우리는 단독으로 있든 섞여 있든 간에 각각의 향을 인지할 수 있어야 한다. 그래서 섬세한 후각을 가진 사람들만이 조향사가 될 수 있다. 이것이 우리가 때때로 '코'라고 불리는 이유이다.
>
> 향수를 만드는 것은 예술 행위이다. 다른 예술가들처럼, 우리는 어떤 감정이나 이미지를 하나의 창작물로 바꾸는데, 이 경우에는 향수가 그것이다. 예를 들어, '열정'과 같은 개념을 위해, 우리는 우선 새로운 '제조법'을 만든다. 이 제조법은 '열정'의 이미지에 맞는 서로 다른 향들과 그것들의 양의 목록이다. 그러고 나서 우리는 매번 각 향기 성분의 양을 바꾸면서 그것들을 여러 번 섞는다. 우리는 적절한 향기를 얻을 때까지 계속해서 제조법을 바꾼다. 이 과정은 몇 달 혹은 몇 년까지도 걸릴 수 있다!
>
> 보다시피, 향수를 만드는 것은 매력적인 일이지만, 그것은 수년간의 훈련을 필요로 한다. 요즈음 일부 사람들은 조향사가 되기 위해 대학 수준의 강의를 듣기도 한다. 하지만 그 사람이 반드시 가지고 있어야 하는 가장 중요한 것은 향수에 대한 애정이다!

어휘 scent[sent] 명 향기, 향내 perfume[pə́:rfju:m] 명 향수 (perfumer 명 조향사, 향수 제조자) spread[spred] 동 퍼지다 fall in love with …에게 반하다 magical[mǽdʒikəl] 형 마력이 있는 mix[miks] 동 섞다 woody[wúdi] 형 나무의 recognize[rékəgnàiz] 동 인지하다, 알아보다 delicate[délikət] 형 연약한; *섬세한 creation[kriéiʃən] 명 창조; *창작품 concept[kánsept] 명 개념 passion[pǽʃən] 명 열정 recipe[résəpi] 명 요리법, 제조법 quantity[kwántəti] 명 양, 분량 ingredient[ingrí:diənt] 명 재료, 성분 fragrance[fréigrəns] 명 향기; 향수 attractive[ətrǽktiv] 형 매력적인 require[rikwáiər] 동 필요로 하다 course[kɔ:rs] 명 강의 absolutely[æbsəlú:tli] 부 절대적으로, 무조건 [문제] aroma[əróumə] 명 향기

構文 1행 ..., and **let** the feeling **spread** through your body.
- 사역동사(let) + 목적어 + 동사원형: …가 ~하게 하다
3행 That's (the reason) **why** I became a perfumer.
- why: 이유를 나타내는 관계부사로, 앞에 선행사 the reason이 생략되어 있음
6행 And we have to be able to recognize each of these scents **whether** alone **or** mixed.
- whether … or ~: …이든 (아니면) ~이든
11행 This recipe is the list of different scents [**that** match the image of "passion"] and their amounts.
- that 이하는 different scents를 수식하는 주격 관계대명사절
18행 But the most important thing [**that** one must absolutely have] is a love for perfume!
- that 이하는 the most important thing을 수식하는 목적격 관계대명사절

STRATEGIC ORGANIZER image, scents, sense, love

EXPANDING KNOWLEDGE

1 faint **2** disgusting **3** perceive **4** odor

어휘 nerve[nəːrv] 명 신경　sight[sait] 명 시력; 보기, 봄　perceive[pərsíːv] 동 인지하다
detect[ditékt] 동 감지하다　odor[óudər] 명 냄새; 악취　stink[stiŋk] 명 악취 동 악취를 풍기다
stench[stentʃ] 명 악취　disgusting[disɡʌ́stiŋ] 형 역겨운, 구역질 나는　faint[feint] 형 희미한
[문제] extremely[ikstríːmli] 부 극도로　become aware of …을 알게 되다

VOCABULARY REVIEW

A　**1** fragrance　**2** attractive　**3** passion　**4** recipe
B　**1** a　**2** d　　C　**1** c　**2** d　**3** c　**4** b

unit
10 MEDICINE pp. 44-47

★Botox

1 c　**2** d　**3** Because it was first found in spoiled sausages.　**4** b　**5** c　**6** 1) T 2) F

독은 우리 주변 어디에나 있다. 우리는 그것을 식물, 동물, 그리고 심지어 몇 종류의 음식에서도 찾아볼 수 있다! 그것은 심각한 해를 끼칠 수 있고, 어떤 것들은 심지어 생명체를 죽일 수도 있다. 하지만 우리에게 예기치 못한 혜택을 주는 독이 있다. 이것은 보톡스라고도 알려진 보툴리누스균이다. 그것은 또한 '소시지 독'이라고도 불리는데, 왜냐하면 그것이 상한 소시지에서 처음 발견되었기 때문이다.

　그것의 별명이 이상하게 들리지만, 보툴리누스균은 세상에서 가장 치명적인 독소들 중 하나이다. 그것은 독성이 너무 강해서, 단 1그램만으로도 백만 명을 죽일 수 있다! 일단 그것이 사람의 몸속에 들어가면, 그것은 서서히 몸 전체의 근육을 마비시킨다. 그것은 얼굴 근육에서 시작해서 팔과 다리로 퍼진다. 그것이 결국 숨을 쉬는 데 사용되는 근육을 기능하지 못하게 하면 사람들은 죽을 수도 있다.

　보툴리누스균은 극도로 위험하지만, 과학자들은 그것이 어떤 질병에 도움이 되는 약이 될 수 있다는 것을 알아냈다. 그들은 그것이 아주 적은 양으로 사용되면, 근육이 수축하는 것을 막을 수 있다는 것을 발견했다! 그래서 이 치명적인 독은 근육병을 치료하는 약이 되었다. 하지만 그것은 또 다른 특별한 효과를 가지고 있다. 1987년에, 캐나다의

한 안과 의사는 눈 주위의 근육에 문제가 있던 한 환자를 치료하기 위해 그것을 사용했다. 그 의사는 그것이 그 문제를 치료했을 뿐만 아니라, 얼굴의 주름도 줄여주었다는 것을 발견하고 놀랐다! 그 이후로, 보톡스는 미용 치료에서 더 인기 있어졌다. 사람들의 목숨을 위협하는 독이 때로는 우리를 도울 수 있다!

어휘   poison[pɔ́izn] 명 독 (poisonous 형 독성이 있는)   spoil[spɔil] 동 망치다; *(음식이) 상하다
nickname[níknèim] 명 별명   fatal[féitl] 형 치명적인   toxin[táksin] 명 독소
gradually[grǽdʒuəli] 부 서서히   paralyze[pǽrəlàiz] 동 마비시키다   muscle[mʌ́sl] 명 근육
dose[dous] 명 복용량, 투여량   contract[kəntrǽkt] 동 줄어들다, 수축하다   treat[tri:t] 동 다루다,
*치료하다 (treatment 명 치료)   eye doctor 안과 의사   cosmetic[kazmétik] 형 미용의,
화장의   threaten[θrétn] 동 협박하다, 위협하다   [문제] disaster[dizǽstər] 명 참사, 재난
unexpected[ʌ̀nikspéktid] 형 예기치 못한   benefit[bénəfit] 명 혜택, 이득   affect[əfékt]
동 영향을 미치다   cure[kjuər] 동 치료하다   reduce[ridjú:s] 동 줄이다   facial[féiʃəl] 형 얼굴의
wrinkle[ríŋkl] 명 주름

구문   7행   It is **so** poisonous **that** just one gram of it can kill one million people!
- so … that ~: 너무 …해서 ~하다
10행   … when it finally **stops** the muscles [*used* for breathing] **from working**.
- stop + 목적어 + from v-ing: …가 ~하지 못하게 막다
- used 이하는 the muscles를 수식하는 과거분사구
14행   So this fatal poison became a medicine **to treat** muscle disease.
- to treat: a medicine을 수식하는 형용사적 용법의 to부정사
17행   The doctor was surprised **to find** that it *not only* cured the problems, *but also* reduced facial wrinkles!
- to find: 감정의 원인을 나타내는 부사적 용법의 to부정사
- not only A but also B: A뿐만 아니라 B도

STRATEGIC ORGANIZER   sausages, Paralyzes, amount, facial

EXPANDING KNOWLEDGE

1 d   **2** *1)* F *2)* T

당신은 동물에서 나오는 일부 독이 당신의 건강에 좋을 수 있다는 것을 알았는가? 칠리안 로즈 타란툴라의 약한 독은 거미에게 별로 유용하지는 않지만, 인간에게 큰 도움이 될 수 있다. 그것에는 심장마비를 막는 데 사용될 수 있는 단백질이 들어 있다. 한편, 전갈은 다른 천연 물질과 섞여 암을 치료하는 약을 만들 수 있는 독을 만들어낸다. 그 새로운 치료제는 매우 장래성이 있어 쿠바 정부는 수천 마리의 전갈을 사육하기 위해 큰 농장들을 만들었다. 그러니 털이 많은 큰 거미나 전갈을 두려워하지 마라. 그것들이 언젠가 당신의 생명을 구할 수도 있다!

어휘   venom[vénəm] 명 (뱀·거미 등의) 독   protein[próuti:n] 명 단백질   heart attack
심장마비   scorpion[skɔ́:rpiən] 명 전갈   promising[prámisiŋ] 형 유망한, 장래성 있는
government[gʌ́vərnmənt] 명 정부   breed[bri:d] 동 새끼를 낳다; *사육하다   be scared of …을
두려워하다   hairy[héəri] 형 털이 많은   [문제] insect[ínsekt] 명 벌레

구문   1행   … some toxins [**that** come from animals] can be good for your health?
- that 이하는 some toxins를 수식하는 주격 관계대명사절
5행   … mixed with other natural substances **to make** a medicine *to treat* cancer.
- to make: 결과를 나타내는 부사적 용법의 to부정사
- to treat: a medicine을 수식하는 형용사적 용법의 to부정사

VOCABULARY REVIEW
A *1* contract *2* treatment *3* paralyze *4* wrinkle
B *1* c *2* a   **C** *1* c *2* d *3* d *4* b

★unit★
11 ISSUES

pp. 48-51

★Flight Fee for the Obese

1 a, c **2** a **3** b **4** b **5** Because obesity is a serious medical condition. **6** c

몇몇 항공사들이 비만인 승객들에게 다른 승객들보다 더 많은 돈을 청구하는 것을 고려해왔다. 그들은 한 좌석에 맞지 않으면 두 좌석을 사야만 할 것이다. 몇몇 학생들이 이 문제에 대해 토론하고 있다.

Robert: 저는 모든 승객이 편안한 여행을 할 권리가 있다고 생각해요. 그리고 체구가 엄청나게 큰 사람들이 옆자리에 앉으면, 당신은 당신의 자리를 함께 써야 하고, 그것은 불편할 수 있어요. 저는 미국의 몇몇 항공사들이 이 이유로 수백 건의 불편 항의를 받았다고 들었어요. 항공사들은 이 문제를 해결하기 위해 뭔가를 해야만 해요!

Sophie: 항공사들은 비만인 고객들을 신경 쓰지 않아요. 이것은 회사들이 해야 할 행동이 아니죠. 그들에게 요금을 더 청구하는 대신, 항공사들은 더 큰 좌석을 제공하도록 노력할 수 있어요! 예를 들어, 캘리포니아의 디즈니랜드는 체구가 더 큰 고객들의 요구를 충족시키기 위해 그들의 놀이기구 좌석을 더 크게 만들었어요. 항공사들은 그들에게 배워야 해요.

Cathy: 하나의 기업으로서, 항공사는 높은 기름값을 고려해야만 해요. 비행기가 무거울수록, 더 많은 기름을 쓰죠. 그것이 그들이 초과 수하물에 대해 더 많은 요금을 청구하는 이유예요. (하지만 초과 수하물의 무게는 항공사마다 달라요.) 그렇다면 사람들에게는 왜 안 되나요? 어떤 사람이 너무 무거워서 항공사가 기름값을 더 내야 한다면, 그 고객이 그 부담을 나누어야 해요!

Daniel: 저는 인간이 수하물에 비교되어서는 안 된다고 생각해요. 너무 뚱뚱하기 때문에 그들에게 요금을 더 청구하는 것은 무례하고 모욕적이에요. 더구나, 많은 경우에 비만은 선택의 문제가 아니에요. 많은 비만인 사람들은 단지 음식에 있어 절제가 부족해서 과체중인 것이 아니에요. 비만은 심각한 질병이에요. 이 사람들은 또 다른 당황스러운 상황이 아니라, 더 많은 배려가 필요해요.

어휘 charge[tʃɑːrdʒ] 동 (요금·값을) 청구하다   obese[oubíːs] 형 비만인 (obesity 명 비만)   fit[fit] 동 (어떤 장소에 들어가기에) 맞다; 맞추다   debate[dibéit] 동 논의하다   issue[íʃuː] 명 문제   right[rait] 명 권리   share[ʃɛər] 동 함께 쓰다; 나누다   discomfort[diskʌ́mfərt] 명 불편 사항   complaint[kəmpléint] 명 불평, 항의   fix[fiks] 동 고정시키다; *(문제를) 바로잡다   care about …에 마음을 쓰다   be supposed to-v …하기로 되어 있다, …해야 한다   ride[raid] 명 놀이기구   excess baggage 초과 수하물   vary[vέəri] 동 다르다, 달라지다   burden[bə́ːrdn] 명 부담, 짐   rude[ruːd] 형 무례한   offensive[əfénsiv] 형 모욕적인   overweight[óuvərwèit] 형 과체중인   lack[læk] 명 부족   when it comes to …에 관한 한   embarrassing[imbǽrəsiŋ] 형 당황스러운 [문제]   profit[práfit] 명 수익   facility[fəsíləti] 명 (pl.) 시설   reasonable[ríːzənəbl] 형 타당한   principle[prínsəpl] 명 원리

구문 7행   I think **every passenger has** the right *to have* a comfortable trip.
• every: '모든'의 의미로, 단수 명사와 함께 쓰여 단수 취급함
• to have: the right를 수식하는 형용사적 용법의 to부정사
8행   …, you have to share your seat, **which** can be uncomfortable.

- which: 앞의 절을 선행사로 하는 계속적 용법의 주격 관계대명사(= and it)

18행 **The heavier** the plane is, **the more** gas it uses.
- the + 비교급 …, the + 비교급 ~: …하면 할수록, 더 ~하다

26행 What's more, in many cases [**being** obese] isn't a matter of choice.
- being 이하는 문장의 주어로 쓰인 동명사구

STRATEGIC ORGANIZER   discomfort, share, care, offensive

EXPANDING KNOWLEDGE

1 substance   **2** lean   **3** flesh   **4** weight

어휘　flesh[fleʃ] 명 살　excessive[iksésiv] 형 지나친, 과도한　nutrition[njuːtríʃən] 명 영양
greasy[gríːsi] 형 기름진　oily[ɔ́ili] 형 기름기가 함유된　store[stɔːr] 동 저장하다　layer[léiər]
명 막, 층　plump[plʌmp] 형 통통한　skinny[skíni] 형 삐쩍 마른　underweight[ʌ̀ndərwéit]
형 표준 체중 이하의　slim[slim] 형 날씬한　lean[liːn] 형 군살이 없는, 호리호리한　slender[sléndər]
형 날씬한　[문제] measurement[méʒərmənt] 명 측정, 측량

VOCABULARY REVIEW

A　**1** excess　**2** charge　**3** debate　**4** offensive
B　**1** a　**2** d　　　**C**　**1** a　**2** d　**3** a　**4** d

unit 12 ANIMALS

pp. 52-55

★ *Voytek*

1 b　**2** b　**3** c　**4** c　**5** They had to enlist him in the Polish army.　**6** b

당신은 제2차 세계대전에 한 용감한 곰이 중요한 역할을 했다는 것을 알았는가? 이것은 Voytek이라는 이름의 곰 병사에 관한 이야기이다.

그 이야기는 1942년에 시작되는데, 그때 이란에 있는 폴란드 군인들이 작은 곰 한 마리를 발견했다. 어미를 잃은 후, 그 곰은 군인들을 자신의 부모라고 생각했다. 그 결과, 그는 인간처럼 행동하기 시작했다. 그는 외로울 때 울고 누군가가 자신에게 소리를 지르면 발로 눈을 가렸다. 그는 또한 맥주를 마시고, 담배를 피우고, 군인들과 레슬링하기를 좋아했다.

그 곰은 폴란드 군인들에게 아주 인기가 많아서 그들의 마스코트가 되었다. 그는 나이가 들면서, 군인들을 돕기 시작했다. 그는 무거운 폭탄과 커다란 탄약 상자들을 날랐는데, 이것은 사람이 혼자서는 절대로 할 수 없었다. 한번은 그가 적군의 스파이를 찾아내기도 했다! 1944년에 군인들이 이탈리아로 보내졌을 때, 그들은 그 곰을 자신들과 함께 데려가고 싶어 했다. 그러나 그것을 할 수 있는 유일한 방법은 그를 폴란드 군대에 입대시키는 것이었다. 그래서 그들은 그에게 이름과 직위, 그리고 군번을 주었다. 그의 이름인 'Voytek'은 '전쟁을 즐기는 자' 또는 '미소 짓는 전사'를 의미한다.

전쟁이 끝난 후, Voytek은 퇴역해 스코틀랜드에 있는 에든버러 동물원으로 보내졌다. 전역한 폴란드 병사들은 때때로 그를 방문해 담배를 던져주었다. 그들은 그가 여전히 폴란드어를 이해할 수 있다고 말했다. Voytek은 1963년에 죽었지만, 그는 절대로 잊혀지지 않을 것이다. 에든버러, 런던, 그리고 오타와에는 Voytek을 기념하는 조각품과 표지판이 있다.

어휘　play a role 역할을 하다　tiny[táini] 형 아주 작은　lonely[lóunli] 형 외로운　paw[pɔː]
명 (동물의 발톱이 달린) 발　shout[ʃaut] 동 소리치다　cigarette[sìɡərét] 명 담배　wrestle[résl]

동 레슬링을 하다　mascot[mǽskət] 명 마스코트　carry[kǽri] 동 나르다　bomb[bam] 명 폭탄
bullet[búlit] 명 총알　enemy[énəmi] 명 적　spy[spai] 명 스파이, 첩자　enlist[inlíst]
동 입대시키다　warrior[wɔ́:riər] 명 전사　retire[ritáiər] 동 은퇴하다　sculpture[skʌ́lptʃər]
명 조각품　sign[sain] 명 징후; *표지판　in memory of …을 기념하여
[문제] intelligence[intélədʒəns] 명 지능

구문　4행　The story begins in 1942, **when** Polish soldiers in Iran found a tiny bear.
　　　　　　• when: 1942를 보충 설명하는 계속적 용법의 관계부사
　　　5행　**Having lost** his mother, the bear *thought of* the soldiers *as* his parents.
　　　　　　• Having lost: 주절의 시제보다 앞선 시점의 내용을 가리키는 완료형 분사구문
　　　　　　• think of A as B: A를 B라고 생각하다
　　　14행　He carried heavy bombs and huge boxes of bullets, **which** a man could never
　　　　　　do alone.
　　　　　　• which: 앞의 절을 선행사로 하는 계속적 용법의 목적격 관계대명사

STRATEGIC SUMMARY　raised, mascot, enlisted, remembered

EXPANDING KNOWLEDGE

1　1) genocide　2) background　3) invasion　　**2**　1) T　2) F

어휘　aftermath[ǽftərmæ̀θ] 명 여파, 후유증　nationalism[nǽʃənəlìzm] 명 민족주의, 애국심
invasion[invéiʒən] 명 침략, 침입　civil war 내전　break out 발발하다　axis[ǽksis] 명 축;
*(제2차 세계 대전 때의) 독일 · 이탈리아 · 일본 추축국　attack[ətǽk] 동 공격하다　advance[ædvǽns]
명 진군　ally[ǽlai] 명 동맹국; *(세계 대전 때의) 연합국　momentum[mouméntəm] 명 탄력, 가속도
collapse[kəlǽps] 동 붕괴되다, 무너지다　impact[ímpækt] 명 영향　casualty[kǽʒuəlti] 명 사상자
concentration camp 강제 수용소　slave labor 강제 노동자　genocide[dʒénəsàid] 명 집단 학살
[문제] murder[mə́:rdər] 명 살인, 살해　by force 강제로　make peace with …와 화해하다

VOCABULARY REVIEW

A　**1** soldier　**2** paw　**3** bullet　**4** sculpture
B　**1** a　**2** b　　　**C**　**1** d　**2** c　**3** b　**4** a

·unit· 13 ENTERTAINMENT pp. 56-59

★Cirque du Soleil

1 a　**2** It was founded in 1984 by two Canadian street performers.　**3** c　**4** a　**5** b　**6** 1) F　2) T

다채로운 조명이 무대를 비추고, 흥겨운 음악이 연주되기 시작하며, 아름다운 의상을 입은 곡예사들이 즐겁게 춤을 추며 무대에 오른다. 쇼가 시작되었다! 당신은 현실에서 걸어 나와 *태양의 서커스*의 황홀한 세계로 들어왔다. 1984년에 두 명의 캐나다 거리 연기자들에 의해 설립된 이 세계적으로 유명한 연예 기획사는 서커스 공연 예술을 완전히 바꾸어 놓았다.
　　그러면 *태양의 서커스*의 독특한 특징들은 무엇인가? 그것은 우스꽝스러운 농담을 하는 광대나 둥근 고리를 점프해서 통과하는 동물이 없다. 대신에, 그것은 고전적인 서커스 공연을 드라마, 춤, 라이브 음악, 그리고 심지어 패션쇼와 같은 다양한 다른 예술적인 요소들과 결합한다. 체조도 또한 결합되며, 곡예사들이 믿을 수 없는 묘기를 선보인다. 그토록 놀라운 공연을 선보이기 위해 *태양의 서커스*는 올림픽 선수들을 포함한 세계 최고의 연기자들을 찾는다!

하지만 더 중요한 것은, 각 공연이 재미있는 줄거리를 가지고 있다는 것이다. 예를 들어, *태양의 서커스*에서 가장 유명한 공연 중 하나인 'Quidam'은 Zoe라는 이름의 소녀에 관한 것이다. 그녀는 지루해하고, 부모의 관심을 얻으려고 애쓰고 있다. (사실, 많은 사람들이 공연 중에 때때로 지루하다고 느낀다.) 그러던 어느 날, Quidam이라고 불리는 한 남자가 그녀를 찾아와 그의 모자를 떨어뜨린다. 그녀가 그 모자를 쓰자, 그녀의 지루한 세계는 다채롭고 활기찬 것으로 변하게 된다.

현재, *태양의 서커스*는 세계 곳곳에서 공연되고 있다. 200개가 넘는 도시에서 약 9천만 명의 사람들이 이 공연의 매력을 경험했다. *태양의 서커스*가 당신의 도시에 왔을 때, 이러한 놀라운 공연들 중 하나를 볼 기회를 놓치지 마라!

어휘   spotlight[spátlàit] 명 환한 조명   merry[méri] 형 즐거운   acrobat[ǽkrəbæt] 명 곡예사   reality[riǽləti] 명 현실   magical[mǽdʒikəl] 형 마법의; *황홀한   world-famous[wə̀:rldféiməs] 형 세계적으로 유명한   entertainment[èntərtéinmənt] 명 오락; *연예   performer[pərfɔ́:rmər] 명 연기자 (performance 명 공연   perform 동 공연하다)   feature[fíːtʃər] 명 특징 동 특징으로 삼다   clown[klaun] 명 광대   silly[síli] 형 바보 같은; *우스꽝스러운   hoop[huːp] 명 고리; *(서커스의 곡예용) 둥근 테   combine[kəmbáin] 동 결합하다   artistic[a:rtístik] 형 예술적인   element[éləmənt] 명 요소   gymnastics[dʒimnǽstiks] 명 체조   unbelievable[ʌnbilíːvəbl] 형 믿기 힘든   trick[trik] 명 속임수; *재주, 묘기   put on …을 입다; *(연극 · 쇼 등을) 무대에 올리다   search for …을 찾다   athlete[ǽθliːt] 명 운동선수   attention[əténʃən] 명 주의, 관심   currently[kə́:rəntli] 부 현재, 지금

구문

4행   This world-famous entertainment company [**founded** in 1984 by two Canadian street performers] *has* completely *changed* the art of circus performance.
- founded 이하는 This world-famous entertainment company를 수식하는 과거분사구
- has changed: '…해 왔다'라는 의미로, 계속을 나타내는 현재완료

7행   It doesn't have clowns [**making** silly jokes] or animals [**jumping** through hoops].
- making과 jumping 이하는 각각 바로 앞의 명사를 수식하는 현재분사구

10행   **Gymnastics is** also mixed in, *with* acrobats *performing* unbelievable tricks.
- Gymnastics: -s로 끝나는 학문명 등은 단수 취급함
- with + 명사 + v-ing: '…가 ～한 채로'라는 의미의 분사구문으로, 명사와 분사가 능동 관계일 때 현재분사를 씀

28행   Don't miss your chance **to see** one of these amazing shows when *Cirque comes* to your city!
- to see: your chance를 수식하는 형용사적 용법의 to부정사
- comes: 시간을 나타내는 부사절에서는 현재시제가 미래시제를 대신함

STRATEGIC ORGANIZER   artistic, talented, story, world-famous

EXPANDING KNOWLEDGE

1 c   **2** *1)* T   *2)* F

라스베이거스에 있을 때, 나는 'O'라고 불리는 *태양의 서커스* 공연을 보았다. 그것은 수중 공연으로, 그 이름인 'O'는 물을 뜻하는 프랑스어 단어인 'eau'에서 유래한다. 극장에서 우리가 처음으로 본 것은 커다란 수영장이었다. 그 공연은 수영장 안과 밖의 아주 멋진 환상의 세계에 대한 것이었다. 수중 발레를 하는 사람들이 공연을 시작했고, 다양한 다른 등장인물들이 그 뒤를 이어 등장했다. 내가 가장 좋아했던 등장인물은 가면을 쓴 도둑이었는데, 그는 불을 가지고 연기를 했다! 나는 또한 음악이 마음에 들었는데, 그 음악은 아프리카 기타와 중국 바이올린과 같은 많은 독특한 악기 소리를 특징으로 했다. 나는 그 공연이 너무 좋아서 그것을 다시 보고 싶다!

어휘   aquatic[əkwǽtik] 형 물속에 사는; *물과 관련된   fantasy[fǽntəsi] 명 공상, 상상   synchronized swimmer 수중 발레를 하는 사람   instrument[ínstrəmənt] 명 기구; *악기

구문　5행　The show was about a magical fantasy world **both** inside **and** outside of the pool.
　　　　• both A and B : A와 B 둘 다
　　　8행　My favorite character was the Masked Thief, **who** played with fire!
　　　　• who: the Masked Thief를 보충 설명하는 계속적 용법의 주격 관계대명사

VOCABULARY REVIEW

A　**1** aquatic　**2** attention　**3** performance　**4** clown
B　**1** d　**2** c　　　C　**1** d　**2** b　**3** b　**4** d

PSYCHOLOGY
pp. 60-63

★Broken Windows Theory

1 d　**2** d　**3** Because an unrepaired broken window makes the building look uncared for.
4 a　**5** b　**6** 1) F　2) T

당신이 쓰레기를 좀 버리고 싶은데 주변에 쓰레기통이 없다고 상상해보라. 그래서 당신은 그냥 쓰레기가 많이 있는 장소에 그것을 버린다. 그 장소는 이미 꽤 더럽기 때문에 그것은 괜찮아 보인다. 이것은 '깨진 유리창 이론'이 어떻게 작용하는지를 보여주는 한 사례이다.

이 이론에 따르면, 어떤 건물의 창문 하나가 깨지고 수리되지 않은 채 방치되면, 나머지 창문들도 곧 깨질 것이라고 한다. 이것은 수리되지 않은 깨진 창문이 그 건물을 관리되지 않는 것처럼 보이게 만들기 때문이다. 이것은 다른 창문들을 깨고 싶어하는 사람들을 유인한다. 이 이론을 시험하기 위해, 한 연구원이 낡은 차 한 대를 가지고 실험을 했다. 그는 길거리에 그 차를 주차했는데, 처음에는 아무도 그것을 건드리지 않았다. 하지만 연구원이 차를 손상시킨 후, 다른 몇몇 사람들이 와서 더 많은 손상을 일으키기 시작했다!

이 이론은 우리에게 무질서가 나쁜 행동을 조장할 수 있다고 말해준다. 비슷하게, 우리가 작은 범죄들을 방치하면, 그것들은 추가적이고 더 심각한 범죄로 이어질 수 있다. 그 시점에는, 너무 늦어서 원래의 '깨진 창문'을 수리하는 것으로는 문제를 해결할 수 없다. 이런 이유로, 뉴욕을 포함한 몇몇 도시의 경찰은 쓰레기 투기나 낙서 같은 작은 범죄에 세심한 주의를 기울인다. 그 결과, 그들은 심각한 범죄의 수를 줄였다. 그러므로 당신은 작은 문제들을 무시하지 말아야 한다. 그렇게 하면, 그것들은 미래에 더 크고 걷잡을 수 없는 문제들로 이어질 수 있다!

어휘　throw away …을 버리다　trash can 쓰레기통　messy[mési] 휑 지저분한　theory[θíːəri] 휑 이론　unrepaired[ʌnripɛ́ərd] 휑 수리되지 않은 (repair 통 수리하다)　rest[rest] 휑 나머지　uncared for 돌보지 않은, 방치된　attract[ətrǽkt] 통 끌다, 유인하다　park[paːrk] 통 주차하다　damage[dǽmidʒ] 통 손상을 주다 휑 손상　disorder[disɔ́ːrdər] 휑 무질서　encourage[inkə́ːridʒ] 통 격려하다; *부추기다, 조장하다　neglect[niglékt] 통 방치하다　minor[máinər] 휑 작은　crime[kraim] 휑 범죄　lead to …로 이어지다　additional[ədíʃənl] 휑 추가의　pay attention to …에 유의하다　litter[lítər] 통 (쓰레기를) 버리다　graffiti[grəfíːti] 휑 낙서　ignore[ignɔ́ːr] 통 무시하다　uncontrollable[ʌnkəntróuləbl] 휑 걷잡을 수 없는　[문제] violence[váiələns] 휑 폭력　proper[prάpər] 휑 적절한　replace[ripléis] 통 대신하다

구문　2행　So you just throw it in a place [**where** there is a lot of trash].
　　　　• where 이하는 a place를 수식하는 관계부사절
　　　5행　This is a case [**that** shows *how the "broken windows theory" works*].
　　　　• that 이하는 a case를 수식하는 주격 관계대명사절
　　　　• how … works: '의문사 + 주어 + 동사' 어순의 간접의문문으로, 동사 shows의 목적어 역할을 함

19

10행   … an unrepaired broken window **makes** the building **look** uncared for.
- 사역동사(make) + 목적어 + 동사원형: …을 ~하게 하다

19행   …, it's **too** late **to solve** the problem by repairing the original "broken window."
- too … to-v: 너무 …해서 ~할 수 없다

STRATEGIC ORGANIZER   unrepaired, attack, serious, focus on

EXPANDING KNOWLEDGE

1 judgment   **2** illegal   **3** criminal   **4** victim

어휘   arrest[ərést] 통 체포하다   criminal[krímənl] 형 범죄의 명 범인, 범죄자   suspect[sʌ́spekt]
명 용의자 통 의심하다   victim[víktim] 명 피해자   illegal[ilíːgəl] 형 불법적인   detective[ditéktiv]
명 형사   evidence[évədəns] 명 증거   judgment[dʒʌ́dʒmənt] 명 판단; 판결   guilty[gílti]
형 유죄의   violation[vàiəléiʃən] 명 위반   offense[əféns] 명 위법 행위, 범죄   misdeed[mìsdíːd]
명 악행   violent[váiələnt] 형 폭력적인   commit[kəmít] 통 저지르다, 범하다   confess[kənfés]
통 자백하다, 고백하다   witness[wítnis] 통 목격하다   [문제] court[kɔːrt] 명 법정

VOCABULARY REVIEW

A   **1** crime   **2** minor   **3** encourage   **4** graffiti
B   **1** a   **2** b   **C**   **1** d   **2** d   **3** c   **4** b

unit 15 CULTURE

pp. 64-67

★*Gross National Happiness*

1 b   **2** c   **3** b   **4** c   **5** c   **6** *1)* T   *2)* F

많은 사람들은 더 많은 것을 가지면 가질수록, 더 행복해질 것이라고 믿는다. 하지만 이것이 사실일까? 그 대답은 부탄에서 찾을 수 있다.

    부탄은 히말라야의 아주 작은 불교 왕국이다. 이곳은 세계에서 가장 덜 발전된 국가 중 하나이고, 대부분의 국민들은 매우 가난하다. (그래서 부탄 사람들은 종교에서 위안을 찾아야 했다.) 하지만 놀랍게도, 부탄은 세계에서 여덟 번째로 가장 행복한 국가이다. 어떻게 이것이 가능할까? 이것은 그들이 국민들의 행복을 측정하기 위해 사용하는 특별한 기준 때문이다. 그것은 국민 총 행복(GNH)이라 불리며, 1972년 부탄의 Wangchuck 왕에 의해 만들어졌다. 그는 물질적인 부가 반드시 행복을 가져오는 것은 아니라고 믿었다. 그래서 그는 다른 방식으로 국민들을 돕기로 결정했고, 경제적인 가치 대신에 그들의 행복에 집중했다.

    GNH를 높이기 위해, 정부는 모든 사람들에게 무료 의료 서비스를 제공함으로써 국민들의 건강을 개선하려고 노력한다. 부탄에서 병을 치료하는 것이 불가능하면, 정부는 그 환자를 외국에 있는 병원으로 보낸다. 게다가, 정부는 국가의 환경과 문화를 보호하기 위해 노력한다. 이것을 하기 위해, 정부는 세심하게 관광업을 규제한다. 관광객들은 허가받은 부탄의 관광업자와 여행사를 통해서만 부탄으로 여행을 갈 수 있다. 또한, 국가의 60퍼센트는 삼림으로 뒤덮여 있어야 한다고 명시하는 법도 있다.

    그러므로 가진 것이 별로 없다고 생각해서 불행하다고 느낄 때마다, 부탄을 기억하라. 행복은 돈에 달린 것이 아니다!

어휘   Buddhist[búːdist] 형 부처의; *불교의   kingdom[kíŋdəm] 명 왕국   developed[divéləpt]
형 발달한, 선진의   refuge[réfjuːdʒ] 명 피난; *위안   religion[rilídʒən] 명 종교
standard[stǽndərd] 명 기준   measure[méʒər] 통 측정하다, 재다   material[mətíəriəl]

⟨형⟩ 물질적인 wealth[welθ] ⟨명⟩ 부, 재산 improve[imprúːv] ⟨동⟩ 개선하다 healthcare[hélθkɛ̀ər]
⟨명⟩ 건강관리, 의료 (서비스) treat[triːt] ⟨동⟩ 대하다; *치료하다 abroad[əbrɔ́ːd] ⟨부⟩ 외국으로
protect[prətékt] ⟨동⟩ 지키다, 보호하다 regulate[régjulèit] ⟨동⟩ 규제하다 tourism[túərizm]
⟨명⟩ 관광업 licensed[láisənst] ⟨형⟩ 허가받은 tour operator 관광업자 agent[éidʒənt]
⟨명⟩ 대리인, 중개인 remain[riméin] ⟨동⟩ 계속 …이다 forested[fɔ́ːristid] ⟨형⟩ 숲으로 뒤덮인
[문제] heritage[héritidʒ] ⟨명⟩ 유산

구문 1행 Many people believe that **the more things** they have, **the happier** they will be.
• the + 비교급 …, the + 비교급 ~: …하면 할수록, 더 ~하다
13행 He believed material wealth does**n't necessarily** bring happiness.
• not necessarily: '반드시[꼭] …은 아니다'라는 의미의 부분부정
17행 If **it**'s impossible [**to treat** an illness in Bhutan], ….
• it은 가주어이고, to treat 이하가 진주어
26행 So **whenever** you feel unhappy because you think ….
• whenever: '…할 때마다'라는 의미의 복합관계부사

STRATEGIC SUMMARY   happiness, poor, measures, improve

EXPANDING KNOWLEDGE

1 1) religion   2) interaction   3) satisfaction   **2**   1) F   2) T

어휘 emotional[imóuʃənl] ⟨형⟩ 감정적인 state[steit] ⟨명⟩ 상태 well-being[wélbíːiŋ] ⟨명⟩ 행복, 웰빙
factor[fǽktər] ⟨명⟩ 요소 influence[ínfluəns] ⟨동⟩ 영향을 미치다 interaction[ìntərǽkʃən]
⟨명⟩ 상호작용 accomplishment[əkámpliʃmənt] ⟨명⟩ 업적, 공적 subjective[səbdʒéktiv]
⟨형⟩ 주관적인 affect[ǽfekt] ⟨명⟩ 정서 ⟨동⟩ 영향을 미치다 satisfaction[sæ̀tisfǽkʃən] ⟨명⟩ 만족
[문제] worship[wɔ́ːrʃip] ⟨명⟩ 예배, 숭배 regardless of …에 상관 없이

VOCABULARY REVIEW

A   **1** kingdom   **2** wealth   **3** create   **4** tourism
B   **1** c   **2** d   C   **1** c   **2** b   **3** a   **4** c

★unit★ 16 MYSTERIES
pp. 68-71

★Winchester House

1 b   **2** The spirits of those who were shot dead by her husband's guns caused her troubles.
3 c   **4** d   **5** d   **6** 1) F 2) T

캘리포니아에는, Winchester House라고 불리는 거대한 저택이 하나 있다. 그것은 그저 아름다운 집처럼 보이지만, 실제로는 유령이 나온다고 여겨진다.
그 집은 1884년 Sarah Winchester에 의해 지어졌다. 그녀의 남편 William은 소총 제조 회사를 소유했다. 그녀는 남편과 딸이 갑작스럽게 병으로 죽기 전에는 행복한 삶을 살았다. 슬픔으로 괴로워하던 중, 그녀는 한 유명한 심령술사로부터 자신의 문제들이 남편의 총에 맞아 죽은 사람들의 영혼들에 의해 일어난 것이라는 말을 들었다. 그 심령술사는 그녀에게 집 한 채를 지어야 하고, 그것을 멈추지 않고 계속 지어야 한다고 말했다. 그래서 그녀는 이 영혼들을 위한 집을 짓기 시작했고, 이후 38년간 매일 그 집에 공을 들였다.

그 집은 많은 이상한 특징들을 가지고 있다. 예를 들어, 거기에는 160개의 방과 약 10,000개의 창문이 있다. 많은 계단들이 천장이나 벽으로 이어지고 수십 개의 비밀 통로들이 있다. 한 계단에는 44개의 계단이 있지만 2미터 정도밖에 올라가지 않는데, 이는 각 계단의 높이가 겨우 5센티미터이기 때문이다. 이러한 특징들에 대해서는 몇 가지 가능한 이유들이 있다. 어떤 사람들은 Winchester 부인이 사악한 영혼들을 혼란스럽게 만들고 싶어 해서 집을 복잡하게 만들었다고 말한다. 다른 사람들은 그녀의 심한 관절염 때문에 그녀가 통증을 덜 느끼도록 집이 설계되었다고 말한다. 이들 중 어느 하나가 사실이든 아니든, 집을 건축하는 동안, 따로 설계도나 실시된 점검이 없었기 때문에, 그 집은 매우 특이해졌다.

요즘에는 전 세계 사람들이 와서 그 집을 본다. 당신도 그 집을 방문하고 싶다면, 조심하라. 관광 가이드가 없다면, 당신은 나오는 길을 결코 찾을 수 없을지도 모른다!

어휘 enormous[inɔ́ːrməs] 형 거대한   mansion[mǽnʃən] 명 대저택   haunted[hɔ́ːntid] 형 유령이 나오는 rifle[ráifl] 명 소총   manufacturing[mæ̀njufǽktʃəriŋ] 형 제조의   suffer[sʌ́fər] 동 시달리다, 고통받다   spirit[spírit] 명 정신; *영혼   shoot[ʃuːt] 동 (총 등을) 쏘다   gun[gʌn] 명 총 work on …에 공을 들이다   staircase[stɛ́ərkèis] 명 계단, 층계   ceiling[síːliŋ] 명 천장 dozens of 수십의, 많은   secret[síːkrit] 형 비밀의   passageway[pǽsidʒwèi] 명 통로 confuse[kənfjúːz] 동 혼동시키다   evil[íːvəl] 형 나쁜, 사악한   complicated[kámpləkèitid] 형 복잡한   severe[sivíər] 형 엄한; *심한   arthritis[ɑːrθráitis] 명 관절염   plan[plæn] 명 계획; *도면, 설계도   inspection[inspékʃən] 명 검사, 점검   construction[kənstrʌ́kʃən] 명 건축 [문제] tragic[trǽdʒik] 형 비극적인   effective[iféktiv] 형 효과적인   escape[iskéip] 동 달아나다, 탈출하다   architect[áːrkətèkt] 명 건축가   relieve[rilíːv] 동 (고통을) 덜어 주다 supervision[sùːpərvíʒən] 명 감독

구문 1행   …, there is an enormous mansion [**called** the Winchester House].
· called 이하는 an enormous mansion을 수식하는 과거분사구
6행   [**While suffering** from sadness], … her troubles were caused by the spirits of those [*who* were shot dead by her husband's guns].
· While suffering 이하는 때를 나타내는 분사구문으로, 의미를 명확하게 하기 위해 접속사를 생략하지 않음
· who 이하는 those를 수식하는 주격 관계대명사절
14행 **Some** say …, so she *made* the house *complicated*. **Others** say ….
· some … others ~: 어떤 사람들은 …, 다른 사람들은 ~
· make + 목적어 + 형용사: …을 ~하게 하다
17행 **Whether or not** either of these is true, there were ….
· whether or not: …이든 아니든

STRATEGIC SUMMARY   haunted, troubles, secret, confuse

EXPANDING KNOWLEDGE

1 evil **2** supernatural **3** soul **4** illusion

어휘 horrifying[hɔ́ːrəfàiiŋ] 형 소름 끼치는   illusion[ilúːʒən] 명 환상, 환각   devil[dévl] 명 악마 soul[soul] 명 영혼   ghost[goust] 명 귀신   superstition[sùːpərstíʃən] 명 미신 supernatural[sùːpərnǽtʃərəl] 형 초자연적인   a restless spirit 죽은 뒤 잠들지 못하는 영혼 [문제] force[fɔːrs] 명 힘, 영향력   spiritual[spíritʃuəl] 형 정신의, 정신적인   separate[sépərət] 형 분리된

VOCABULARY REVIEW

A **1** severe **2** haunted **3** horrifying **4** secret
B **1** c **2** c   C **1** b **2** d **3** c **4** b

★*unit* ★
17 TECHNOLOGY pp. 72-75

★*Brain-Computer Interface*

1 a **2** d **3** c **4** They are working on ways for people to operate television sets and cellphones just by thinking. **5** b **6** *1)* F *2)* T

> *마이너리티 리포트*라는 영화를 본 적이 있는가? 거기에는, 컴퓨터가 인간의 뇌파를 감지하는 장면이 있다. 그러고 나서 그것은 그 사람이 생각하고 있는 것을 화면에 보여준다. 당신은 이것이 공상에 불과하다고 생각할 수도 있다. 그러나 그것은 사실 그렇게 비현실적인 것이 아닌데, 왜냐하면 현재 인간의 뇌파를 읽을 수 있는 기술이 있기 때문이다!
>
> 그 기술은 뇌 컴퓨터 인터페이스 또는 BCI라고 불린다. 그것은 사람의 뇌를 컴퓨터에 연결하는 방식이다. 이 시스템이 작동하기 위해 과학자들은 사람의 뇌에 특수한 칩을 부착한다. <u>이 칩은 뇌의 신호를 감지하고 그것을 컴퓨터로 보낸다.</u> 그러면 컴퓨터가 신호의 의미를 해석하고 장치에 할 일을 명령한다. 이런 방식으로, 사람은 자신의 생각으로 장치를 통제할 수 있다. BCI를 사용해서, 사람들은 이미 편지를 쓰거나 컴퓨터 게임을 할 수 있다. 과학자들은 이제 사람들이 생각만으로 텔레비전 수상기와 휴대전화를 작동시키는 방식에 대해 연구하고 있다.
>
> 그러나 이 기술은 단지 편리하고 재미있기 때문에 관심을 끄는 것이 아니다. 게다가 그것은 <u>장애인들에게 희망을 준다.</u> 예를 들어, 로봇 팔이나 다리는 사람의 신체에 부착될 수 있다. 그러고 나서, BCI를 사용해서 그 사람은 그것을 움직이는 생각을 반복적으로 한다. 결국, 로봇 장치는 주인이 원할 때 움직이는 것을 '배우게 된다'. 미래에, 이것은 마비된 사람들을 스스로 걸을 수 있게 할지도 모른다!

어휘 scene[siːn] 명 장면 sense[sens] 동 느끼다; *(기계가)* 감지하다 brainwave[bréinwèiv] 명 뇌파 screen[skriːn] 명 화면, 스크린 fantasy[fǽntəsi] 명 환상, 공상 unrealistic[ʌ̀nriːəlístik] 형 비현실적인 technology[teknάlədʒi] 명 기술 connect[kənékt] 동 연결하다 attach[ətǽtʃ] 동 부착하다 interpret[intə́ːrprit] 동 해석하다 signal[sígnəl] 명 신호 device[diváis] 명 (기계) 장치 control[kəntróul] 동 통제하다, 조종하다 operate[άpərèit] 동 작동[가동]시키다 draw attention 주의를 끌다 convenient[kənvíːnjənt] 형 편리한 (convenience 명 편리) eventually[ivéntʃuəli] 부 결국 paralyzed[pǽrəlàizd] 형 마비된 [문제] advanced[ædvǽnst] 형 진보된 automatic[ɔ̀ːtəmǽtik] 형 자동의 detect[ditékt] 동 발견하다, 감지하다 cure[kjuər] 동 치유하다

구문
1행 In it, there is a scene [**where** a computer senses a human's brainwaves].
  • where 이하는 a scene을 수식하는 관계부사절
2행 Then it shows **what** the person is thinking on a screen.
  • what: '…하는 것'의 의미로, 선행사를 포함하는 관계대명사
4행 …, because there is now technology [**that** can read people's brainwaves]!
  • that 이하는 technology를 수식하는 주격 관계대명사절
12행 Now scientist are working on ways **for people** *to operate* ….
  • for people: to부정사의 의미상 주어
  • to operate: ways를 수식하는 형용사적 용법의 to부정사
17행 Eventually, the robotic device "learns" to move when its owner **wants** it **to** (move).
  • want + 목적어 + to-v: …가 ~하기를 원하다
  • to: to move를 대신하는 대부정사로, 뒤에 반복되는 부분인 move가 생략됨

STRATEGIC SUMMARY thinking, attaching, convenient, paralyzed

23

EXPANDING KNOWLEDGE

1 *1)* process *2)* protection *3)* perception   **2** *1)* T *2)* F

어휘   division[divíʒən] 명 분할; 구획 (divide 동 나누다)   skull[skʌl] 명 두개골   protection[prətékʃən]
명 보호   function[fʌ́ŋkʃən] 명 기능   process[práses] 동 처리하다   perception[pərsépʃən]
명 지각   metabolism[mətǽbəlìzm] 명 신진대사   stroke[strouk] 명 타격; *뇌졸중
tumor[tjú:mər] 명 종양   syndrome[síndroum] 명 증후군   [문제] deal with (문제·과제 등을)
처리하다   have nothing to do with …와 관계가 없다

VOCABULARY REVIEW

A 1 automatic **2** convenient **3** attach **4** device
B 1 b **2** c   **C 1** c **2** d **3** b **4** c

★unit★
18 ENVIRONMENT
pp. 76-79

★Light Pollution

1 c **2** d **3** b **4** b **5** It has encouraged governments to change laws about lighting and
introduce better lighting systems.   **6** *1)* T *2)* F

당신은 시골에서 별들을 올려다본 적이 있는가? 그것들은 멋져 보인다! 하지만 도시에서 당신은 아마 어떤 별도 볼 수
없을 것이다. 왜 그럴까? 우리가 별들을 보는 것을 어렵게 만드는 것은 바로 밝은 불빛들이다. 이 문제는 광공해라고
불린다. 그것은 가로등, 네온사인, 그리고 우리의 가정에서 나오는 불빛과 같은 것들에 의해 일어난다.

하지만 별을 보지 못하는 것이 유일한 문제는 아니다. 광공해는 심각한 건강 문제들도 일으킨다. 그것은 심지어
유방암과 연관되어 있다. 과학자들에 따르면, 광공해는 우리의 몸이 유방암과 싸우는 중요한 화학물질인 멜라토닌을
충분히 만들어내지 못하게 한다. 광공해는 또한 어떤 사람들에게는 정상적으로 수면을 취하지 못하게 하고, 다른
사람들에게는 고혈압을 일으킨다.

광공해는 또한 환경에도 나쁘다. 모든 생물들은 빛과 어둠의 자연스러운 균형에 의존한다. 너무 많은 인공 불빛은
식물의 성장을 방해하고 그것들의 생명을 위협할 수 있다. (꽃이 죽으면, 열매가 자라기 시작한다.) 게다가, 필요 이상의
불빛은 동물들, 특히 밤에 활동하는 동물들을 혼란스럽게 만들 수 있다. 그것은 또한 그들의 번식 능력에 영향을 미친다.

그러면, 이 문제를 해결하기 위해 무엇이 행해지고 있는가? 국제 밤하늘 보호 협회(IDA)는 정부들에 조명에 대한
법규를 바꾸고 더 나은 조명 장치를 도입할 것을 권장해 왔다. 그 결과, 이탈리아에 있는 많은 도시들이 빛이 옆과
위로 새어나가지 못하게 하기 위해 가로등을 교체했다. 만약 더 많은 곳이 그와 같은 노력을 기울인다면, 우리는 모두
아름다운 별들을 다시 볼 수 있게 될 것이다!

어휘   countryside[kʌ́ntrisàid] 명 시골 지역   pollution[pəlú:ʃən] 명 오염, 공해   link[liŋk] 동 관련 짓다
breast cancer 유방암   chemical[kémikəl] 명 화학물질   normally[nɔ́:rməli] 부 정상적으로
blood pressure 혈압   balance[bǽləns] 명 균형   hinder[híndər] 동 방해하다   threaten[θrétn]
동 협박[위협]하다   confuse[kənfjú:z] 동 혼란시키다   active[ǽktiv] 형 활동적인   breed[bri:d]
동 새끼를 낳다, 번식하다   encourage[inkə́:ridʒ] 동 격려하다; *권장하다   escape[iskéip] 동 탈출하다;
*새어 나가다   sideways[sáidwèiz] 부 옆으로   upwards[ʌ́pwərdz] 부 위쪽으로

구문   4행   **It is** the bright lights **that** make *it* hard **for us** [*to see* stars].
• It is ... that ~: '~한 것은 바로 …이다'의 의미로, the bright lights를 강조하는 강조구문
• it은 가목적어이고, to see 이하가 진목적어
• for us: to부정사의 의미상 주어

24

7행   But **not seeing the stars** is not the only problem.
- not seeing the stars: 주어로 쓰인 동명사구로, 동명사구의 부정은 동명사 앞에 not을 붙임

9행   …, light pollution **stops** our bodies **from producing** enough *melatonin*, *an important chemical* [**that** fights breast cancer].
- stop + 목적어 + from v-ing: …가 ～하지 못하게 하다
- melatonin과 an important chemical은 동격
- that 이하는 an important chemical을 수식하는 주격 관계대명사절

STRATEGIC ORGANIZER   Bright, risk, sleeping, plants

EXPANDING KNOWLEDGE

1 *1)* disaster   *2)* emission   *3)* protocol   **2** *1)* T *2)* F

어휘   fossil fuel 화석 연료   emission[imíʃən] 명 배출물, 배출가스   wastewater[wéistwɔ̀ːtər] 명 폐수, 오수   natural disaster 자연재해   excessive[iksésiv] 형 과도한   soil[sɔil] 명 흙, 땅   pesticide[péstisàid] 명 살충제   reduce[ridjúːs] 동 줄이다, 축소하다   reuse[riːjúːz] 동 재사용하다   recycle[riːsáikl] 동 재활용하다   protocol[próutəkɔ̀ːl] 명 협정   [문제] release[rilíːs] 동 방출하다   arrangement[əréindʒmənt] 명 합의, 협의   coal[koul] 명 석탄   pollute[pəlúːt] 동 오염시키다

VOCABULARY REVIEW

A *1* breed *2* pollution *3* active *4* government
B *1* c *2* a   **C** *1* d *2* b *3* d *4* c

unit 19 MYTHOLOGY   pp. 80-83

★*Odin*

1 d   **2** d   **3** They help him by flying around and telling him about what is happening.   **4** c
5 b   **6** b

우리는 그리스와 로마의 전설에 대해서는 많이 알고 있지만, 북유럽의 전설에 대해서는 그렇지 않다. 하지만 산타클로스와 간달프 같은 몇몇 유명한 가상의 인물들은 북유럽 전설의 신(神)들 중 하나인 오딘에 바탕을 두고 있다. 그의 이름이 익숙지 않게 들릴 수도 있지만, 수요일은 사실 이 이름의 다른 철자인 Woden에서 비롯한다. 그러면 오딘은 누구인가?

오딘은 북유럽 전설에서 가장 위대한 신으로, 그의 중요성은 그리스의 최고 신인 제우스의 그것에 비교될 수 있다. 이 전설에 따르면, 그의 능력은 무한하고 그의 권력은 상상할 수 없다. 그는 전쟁, 마술, 그리고 심지어 죽음도 지배한다. 그는 미래를 말할 수 있고, 자기 자신을 동물이나 다른 모습으로 바꿀 수 있다. 게다가, 그에게는 날아다니며 무슨 일이 일어나고 있는지를 말해주어 그가 세상을 지배하도록 돕는 두 마리의 까마귀가 있다. 그는 또한 위대한 전사이며 다리가 여덟 개 달린 말을 타고 전쟁에 나간다.

오딘은 또한 지혜에 대한 대단한 열정을 가지고 있다. 많은 전설들이 지혜에 대한 오딘의 끊임없는 탐구에 대해 이야기한다. 한 이야기에서, 그는 마법의 우물에서 지혜의 음료를 얻기 위해 한쪽 눈을 포기했다. <u>눈을 잃은 후, 오딘은 훨씬 더 무모한 탐색을 시도했다.</u> 그는 더 현명해지기 위해서 마법 나무에 목을 매닮으로써 9일 동안 죽어 있었다. 이러한 노력을 통해, 그는 많은 지식을 얻었다. 그것이 오딘이 <u>지혜의 신</u>이라고도 불리는 이유이다!

어휘   legend[lédʒənd] 명 전설   imaginary[imǽdʒənèri] 형 가상의   unfamiliar[ʌ̀nfəmíljər] 형 익숙지 않은, 낯선   spelling[spéliŋ] 명 맞춤법; *철자   chief[tʃiːf] 형 주된; *최고의   limitless[límitlis]

⊛ 무한한   rule[ruːl] ⊛ 통치하다, 지배하다   warrior[wɔ́ːriər] ⊛ 전사   battle[bǽtl] ⊛ 전투 passion[pǽʃən] ⊛ 열정 (passionate ⊛ 열정적인)   endless[éndlis] ⊛ 무한한, 한없는 wisdom[wízdəm] ⊛ 지혜   well[wel] ⊛ 우물   hang[hæŋ] ⊛ 목을 매달다   [문제] fortune-teller[fɔ́ːrtʃəntèlər] ⊛ 점쟁이   reckless[réklis] ⊛ 무모한   quest[kwest] ⊛ 탐구, 탐색

구문   1행   We know much about the legends of Greece and Rome but not about **those** of Northern Europe.
· those: the legends를 대신하는 대명사

6행   Odin is the greatest god in Northern European legends, **whose** importance can be compared to *that* of Zeus, the chief Greek god.
· whose: the greatest god을 선행사로 하는 계속적 용법의 소유격 관계대명사
· that: importance를 대신하는 대명사

13행   …, he has two ravens [**that** *help* him *rule* over the world by flying around and telling him about **what is happening**].
· that 이하는 two ravens를 수식하는 주격 관계대명사절
· help + 목적어 + 동사원형: …가 ~하도록 돕다
· what is happening: '의문사(주어) + 동사' 어순의 간접의문문으로, 전치사 about의 목적어 역할을 함

STRATEGIC SUMMARY   imaginary, chief, abilities, wisdom

EXPANDING KNOWLEDGE

1 reasonable   **2** counsel   **3** philosophy   **4** judgment

어휘   awareness[əwέərnis] ⊛ 의식   insight[ínsàit] ⊛ 통찰력, 이해   philosophy[filásəfi] ⊛ 철학 depth[depθ] ⊛ 깊이   judgment[dʒʌ́dʒmənt] ⊛ 판단   reasonable[ríːzənəbl] ⊛ 타당한, 사리에 맞는   knowledgeable[nálidʒəbl] ⊛ 아는 것이 많은   ignorant[ígnərənt] ⊛ 무지한 investment[invéstmənt] ⊛ 투자   counsel[káunsəl] ⊛ 조언   [문제] fair[fɛər] ⊛ 공정한, 공평한 practical[prǽktikəl] ⊛ 실질적인; 실용적인; *타당한   sensible[sénsəbl] ⊛ 분별 있는, 합리적인 formally[fɔ́ːrməli] ⊛ 공식적으로   existence[igzístəns] ⊛ 존재   conclusion[kənklúːʒən] ⊛ 결론

VOCABULARY REVIEW

A   **1** quest   **2** legend   **3** warrior   **4** well
B   **1** c   **2** d   C   **1** d   **2** a   **3** b   **4** c

★*unit*★
20 MATHEMATICS   pp. 84-87

★*Leonardo Fibonacci*

1 c   **2** c   **3** Because he brought it to the West from India.   **4** a   **5** b   **6** *1)* T   *2)* F

1, 2, 3, 4 …. 당신도 알다시피, 이 숫자들은 아라비아 숫자라고 불린다. 이러한 종류의 숫자 체계는 중세에 피보나치라는 이름의 이탈리아 수학자에 의해 유럽으로 전해졌다. 그때까지, 사람들은 로마 숫자를 사용했는데, 그것은 그리 실용적이지 않았다. (그럼에도 불구하고, 로마 숫자는 오늘날 여전히 사용되고 있으며 많은 장소에서 발견될 수 있다.) 피보나치는 모든 수들이 단 10개의 숫자만으로 쓰일 수 있다는 것을 보여주었는데, 이 숫자들은 사물을 계산하기 위해 쉽게 이동되고 바뀔 수 있다. 이것은 현대 수학의 기초를 제공해 주었다.

그는 또한 이 수열을 개발했다: 1, 1, 2, 3, 5, 8, 13, 21, 34, 55, 89, 144 …. 그것은 피보나치 수열이라고 불리며, 각 숫자는 그 앞의 두 숫자를 더해서 만들어진다. 사실, 이 수열을 발견한 사람은 피보나치가 아니었다. 그가 그것을 인도에서 서양으로 가지고 왔기 때문에 그것은 그의 이름을 따서 명명되었다. 피보나치 수열은 자연에 있는 많은 것들을 설명한다. 예를 들어, 꽃의 꽃잎과 식물의 잎의 수는 피보나치 수열을 따른다. 그것이 우리가 1개, 2개, 3개, 5개의 꽃잎을 가진 꽃을 쉽게 찾을 수 있는 이유이다. 하지만 행운의 네 잎 클로버와 같이 4개의 꽃잎을 가진 꽃과 4개의 잎을 가진 식물은 매우 드물다.

당신이 볼 수 있듯이, 피보나치는 수학에 많은 위대한 기여를 했다. 그는 여전히 세계에서 가장 위대한 수학자들 중 한 명으로 여겨진다. 그가 없었더라면, 수학은 오늘날과 똑같지 않을 것이다!

어휘 numeral[njú:mərəl] 명 숫자   mathematician[mæθəmətíʃən] 명 수학자   calculate[kǽlkjulèit]
동 계산하다   provide[prəváid] 동 제공하다   basis[béisis] 명 근거; *기반   sequence[sí:kwəns]
명 순서; *수열   add[æd] 동 더하다   discover[diskʌ́vər] 동 발견하다   petal[pétəl]
명 꽃잎   uncommon[ʌnkámən] 형 드문   contribution[kàntrəbjú:ʃən] 명 기여, 이바지
[문제] formula[fɔ́:rmjulə] 명 공식

구문 4행 Up until then, people **had used** Roman numerals, *which* were not very practical.
• had used: 과거 기준 시점까지 계속된 상태나 동작을 나타내는 과거완료
• which: Roman numerals를 보충 설명하는 계속적 용법의 주격 관계대명사
13행 Actually, **it was not** Fibonacci **who** discovered this sequence.
• it was not … who[that] ~: '~한 것은 …가 아니었다'의 의미로, Fibonacci를 강조하는 강조구문
18행 That's (the reason) **why** we can easily find flowers ….
• why: 이유를 나타내는 관계부사로, 앞에 선행사 the reason이 생략되어 있음
24행 **Without him**, mathematics **would**n't **be** the same today!
• '(과거에) …이 없었다면, (지금) ~할 텐데'라는 의미의 혼합가정법으로, without이 이끄는 구가 if절을 대신함(= If it had not been for him)

STRATEGIC SUMMARY   Arabic, sequence, sum, nature

EXPANDING KNOWLEDGE

1 accuracy   **2** subtract   **3** total   **4** angle

어휘 figure[fígjər] 명 숫자   evaluate[ivǽljuèit] 동 평가하다   angle[ǽŋgl] 명 각도
accuracy[ǽkjurəsi] 명 정확, 정확도   subtract[səbtrǽkt] 동 빼다   multiply[mʌ́ltəplài] 동 곱하다
divide[diváid] 동 나누다   estimate[éstəmèit] 동 추정하다   count[kaunt] 동 세다; *계산하다
compute[kəmpjú:t] 동 계산하다   average[ǽvəridʒ] 명 평균   [문제] exact[igzǽkt] 형 정확한
correct[kərékt] 형 옳은   straight[streit] 형 곧은, 똑바른   degree[digrí:] 명 (각도의 단위인) 도

VOCABULARY REVIEW

A **1** sequence   **2** numeral   **3** petal   **4** basis
B **1** a **2** b   C **1** d **2** c **3** d **4** d

MEMO

MEMO

MEMO

MEMO

MEMO